The Antarctic Treaty System:
Politics, Law, and Diplomacy

D1617204

ABOUT THE BOOK AND AUTHOR

Because negotiations for the Antarctic Treaty were kept secret, the issues that shaped the treaty system have been poorly understood. Dr. Myhre breaks new ground by examining the records of the first Antarctic Treaty Consultative Meetings and evaluating the events of the Special Consultative Meetings on Antarctic Mineral Resources.

Introducing the reader to Antarctic politics, Dr. Myhre examines legal and political problems arising from some nations' claims to sovereignty in Antarctica, reviews initial efforts to create an international administration for the region, and studies in detail the terms of the treaty and the rules of procedure for the consultative meetings. Turning to the diplomatic events that molded the treaty system, he concentrates on the issues that emerged in the 1960s: conservation, the role of Meetings of Experts, the position of the Scientific Committee on Antarctic Research within the treaty system, the obligations of acceding states to uphold previous agreements, and the Consultative Powers' failure to establish an Antarctic Secretariat. Finally, he reviews the two main challenges to the system's survival—mineral extraction and Third World opposition to the present structure.

Jeffrey D. Myhre is a free-lance writer and a former editor of *Millennium: Journal of International Studies*.

The Antarctic Treaty System: Politics, Law, and Diplomacy

Jeffrey D. Myhre

Westview Press / Boulder and London

Westview Special Studies in International Relations

This Westview softcover edition was manufactured on our own premises using equipment and methods that allow us to keep even specialized books in stock. It is printed on acid-free paper and bound in softcovers that carry the highest rating of the National Association of State Textbook Administrators, in consultation with the Association of American Publishers and the Book Manufacturers' Institute.

Published in 1986 in the United States of America by Westview Press, Inc.; Frederick A. Praeger, Publisher; 5500 Central Avenue, Boulder, Colorado 80301

Library of Congress Cataloging-in-Publication Data
Myhre, Jeffrey D.
  The Antarctic Treaty system.
  (Westview special studies in international relations)
  Bibliography: p.
  Includes index.
  1. Antarctic regions—International status.
2. Mining law—Antarctic regions. I. Title. II. Series.
JX4084.A5M97 1986   341.2'9'09989   86-15842
ISBN 0-8133-7286-0

Composition for this book was provided by the author.
This book was produced without formal editing by the publisher.

Printed and bound in the United States of America

The paper used in this publication meets the requirements of the American National Standard for Permanence of Paper for Printed Library Materials Z39.48-1984.

6   5   4   3   2   1

CONTENTS

ACKNOWLEDGMENTS

No book is the result of the solitary efforts of the author. This is especially true of scholarly works and of this book in particular. Therefore, I cannot accept all of the credit for this study as many people assisted me in creating it.

Most of all, my parents are responsible for the completion of this project. They taught me to do whatever I was interested in doing and to do it as well as I could. Without their support and example, this work would never have begun.

Academically, Marjorie McIntosh, E. Christian Kopff, Charles Middleton, Michael Banks, Peter J. Beck and Carlos Moneta were all of enormous help. When I was an undergraduate, I learned how research was truly done from Drs. McIntosh and Kopff and Dean Middleton. Michael Banks helped with invaluable suggestions and criticisms in the early stages of my research and thereby saved me months of futile effort. Moreover, he did not let me quit, and he had the honesty to tell me when I was making mistakes. Drs. Beck and Moneta also gave me valuable advice and a sense of camaraderie in our common, but in no sense commonplace, field of research.

My friends were all a priceless source of support throughout, and beyond, the writing of this book. To Will Carpenter, Andrew McNicholas, Carla Garpedian, Hillary Sale, Mark Hoffman, Jane Merriman, Hilary Parker, Mark Schaffer, Evelyn Karlsberg, Lisha Haan, Peter Walsh, Greg Matera, Julie Baitlon, Leslie Lyons, Nicole Dillenberg, and Charlotte Heller, I can only say thank you one and all.

I would also like to express my gratitude to the London School of Economics and Political Science, the University of London and the University of Colorado for the academic environments that they provided.

Further thanks go to Alison Wilson of the Polar Archives at the US National Archives, R. Tucker Scully of the US Department of State, Jim Barnes of the Antarctica Project, Roger Wilson of Greenpeace, Barbara Ellington of Westview Press, and Lord Shackleton.

If I have overlooked anyone who contributed in one way or another, I apologize.

Although all of these people helped me along in their various ways, my name is on the title page. They supplied me with the support and information, but I must take full responsibility for what I did with it. Whatever shortcomings this book may possess are entirely my own doing.

Jeffrey D. Myhre
Englewood, Colorado

ix

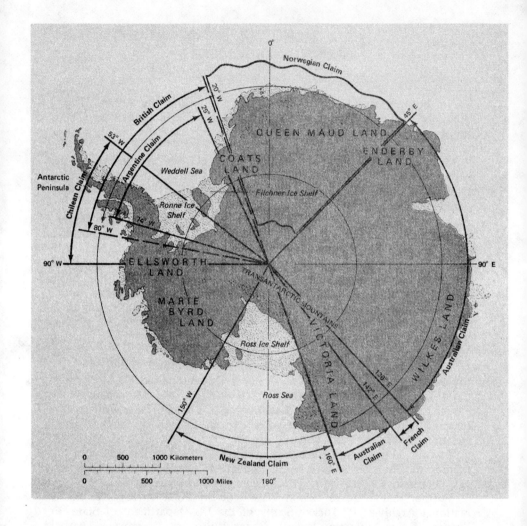

Territorial Claims

Source: Reprinted by permission from *A Pole Apart: The Emerging Issue of Antarctica* by Philip W. Quigg, p. 111 (New York: New Press, McGraw-Hill, 1983). © 1983 by the Twentieth Century Fund.

CHAPTER I
AN OVERVIEW

The conventional wisdom holds that a treaty, once signed and ratified, represents the end of an international problem. Like most conventional beliefs, this is inaccurate. Once a treaty is concluded, the legal and diplomatic formula embodied in the agreement must be made to function in the real world of international politics and economics. It must be adapted to the prevailing world situation, and it must continue to adapt as that situation changes over time. Simply, it must evolve, much as an organism does, to cope with its environment. A treaty that fails to evolve is soon abrogated or ignored. As implied by the title, the purpose of this study is to examine how and to what extent the Antarctic Treaty and its supporting agreements and arrangements (collectively, the Antarctic Treaty System) overcame the early challenges to their survival as well as to look at the present and future challenges the System faces.

To a certain degree, geophysical considerations have influenced the politics of Antarctica. It is the coldest and highest continent with winter winds commonly exceeding 100 kilometers per hour. An ice-sheet averaging over a mile thick covers about 95 per cent of Antarctica, and the ice extends into the adjacent sea. Even in summer, ice-breakers are sometimes needed to aid other vessels in the area.[1] In light of this, it comes as no surprise that Antarctica's human inhabitants are scientists, explorers and support staff residing there only temporarily; there is no indigenous human population. Consequentially, the anti-colonialism of the past decades has passed Antarctica by leaving some states with claims to territorial sovereignty in the region. In part due to this sparse population and in part due to simple inaccessibility, the area's economic resources have not been exploited to any great degree. Thus, unlike most of the rest of the world, Antarctic politics has been more influenced by research science than by economic interests.

That said, there are three other subjects to understand before any informed discussion of the Antarctic Treaty System can begin: 1) territorial sovereignty under international law, 2) the history of Antarctic exploration as it relates to territorial claims and 3) the events that led to the Washington Conference of 1959 where the Antarctic Treaty was signed.

Because of Antarctica's lack of an indigenous human population, the relevant body of international law on territoriality is that pertaining to the acquisition of unoccupied lands. Numerous principles are included in this field, e.g., inchoate title acquired by virtue of discovery, actual displays of sovereignty and *animus occupandi*. All of these can be easily and clearly explained by the brief examination of a few international legal decisions: the Island of Palmas Case, the Clipperton Island Award and the Legal Status of Eastern Greenland Case.

Once the general principles concerning sovereignty are understood, they must be applied to the specific case of Antarctic territorial claims. Therefore, a short examination of the history of Antarctic exploration is in order. This will give the reader an idea of what existing claims to sovereignty in the region are valid, which ones are suspect and what future claims may legitimately be advanced by states that have, as yet, no claim in Antarctica (Chapter II).

Next, it is necessary to understand the origins of the Antarctic Treaty and its peripheral agreements. As a direct result of tensions over territorial claims to Antarctica, the United States government undertook efforts to settle the existing disputes. Fearing a split among America's allies over rival claims shortly after World War II, the State Department circulated draft agreements to the states involved, and these states, in turn, offered their criticisms. This interaction demonstrates some of the thinking in Washington and elsewhere that would eventually lead to the Antaractic Treaty of 1959. At almost the same time, scientific efforts in the Antarctic surged, and the influence of research science on the Antarctic System began. Although the records of the Washington Conference remain classified, the Treaty itself, when contrasted with the proposals that preceded it, shows how the situation developed during the 1950s (Chapter III).

Because the Antarctic Treaty forms the foundation of the Antarctic System and because the Treaty's supporting agreements sprang directly from the 1959 agreement, an article-by-article look at the Treaty is vital to understanding the System and its evolution (Chapter IV, and for the full text of the Treaty itself, see Appendix A).

As provided for in Article IX of the Treaty, the signatories began holding more or less regular Consultative Meetings to address the issues that arose from efforts to implement the Treaty. In the early years, these issues fell into three categories: 1) environmental issues, 2) technical structures and 3) political arrangements.[2] In the period under consideration, 1961-1968, the signatories of the Antarctic Treaty were addressing the most fundamental issues and the ones of most significance in the adaptation of the Treaty to the world of international politics. Although later years held far more noteworthy successes than the first years of the System, the diplomacy of the 1960s laid the groundwork for the functioning of the System. Common sense makes it clear that the initial challenges to the agreement's survival were the most critical, and it is a credit to those involved that the disputes between the signatory states were resolved without resort to a compromise that would undermine the Treaty. That the later successes were possible is in large part the result of meeting the early challenges successfully.

In the field of conservation, the Treaty expressly mandates Consultative Meetings for the "preservation and conservation of living resources in Antarctica."[3] Thus, the Meetings from the beginning, in 1961, concerned themselves with protecting the Antarctic environment. Because of the extreme climate, the Antarctic ecosystems are particularly vulnerable to outside interference, and human activities in the region definitely fit this description. By the end of the Third Consultative Meeting in 1964, the Consultative Meetings had passed Recommendations to the participating governments covering such questions as the importation of non-indigenous species, parasites and diseases, the establishment of Specially Protected Areas[4] and provisions for the protection of pelagic seals.[5] The latter quite clearly is the forebearer of the 1972 Convention on Pelagic Sealing. Additionally, the 1980 Convention on the Conservation of Antarctic Marine Living Resources has its roots in the initial efforts on conservation begun in 1961 (Chapter V).

As for matters of technical structure, these issues addressed the integration of scientific interests and expertise into the System. This is significant because the main industry of Antarctica is the production of scientific data, and the System had to accomodate this if it were to survive. In particular, the role of the Scientific Committee on Antarctic Research (SCAR) had to be determined as well as the role of Meetings of Scientific Experts.

Born during the preparations for the International Geophysical Year as the Special Committee on Antarctic Research, SCAR is a non-governmental organization designed to coordinate scientific research between scientists from different countries. Clearly, this group had to have some sort of technical role within the Antarctic System, but at the same time, there were efforts by various signatory governments to delegate non-scientific duties upon SCAR, and they seem to continue into the 1980s (Chapter VI).

In addressing the role of Meetings of Experts, the signatory powers had to decide whether agreements made by scientists at scientific meetings would have the same status, and therefore the same legal significance, as those made by diplomats at diplomatic meetings. In other words, they had to establish whether there was any difference between Consultative Meetings, called to address the issues of concern, and Meetings of Experts called to discuss matters of scientific importance. This clash between scientific and administrative needs is one of the distinguishing features of Antarctic politics (Chapter VI).

In the case of political arrangements, these problems dealt directly with the administration and enforcement of the System's rules and decisions. If these problems could not have been resolved, the System would almost certainly have collapsed within a few years. During the 1960s, these issues were: 1) the Duties of Acceding States with regard to Recommendations in force and 2) the establishment of an Antarctic secretariat.

Under Article XII, any state may accede to the Treaty, subject to a few reservations. However, the Recommendations (i.e., the rules and regulations passed by the signatories at Consultative Meetings) of previous Meetings were not included as part of the Treaty itself. Thus, it would be possible for a state to join the Treaty System while rejecting such Recommendations as it chose. This would obviously have destroyed the System in short order. The protection of the System from this sort of attack was addressed and settled at the first three Consultative Meetings (Chapter VIII).

The other matter of political concern, the establishment of an Antarctic bureaucracy, arose because of a perceived need for a centralized administration in the policies of certain governments. However, such proposals threatened to call into question territorial rights, cause greater politicization of the System and create the usual difficulties encountered with international bureaucracy (Chapter IX).

Having concluded the examination of the System's past achievements and failures, the study turns to the present and future. The next few years pose two significant problems for the Antarctic Treaty System: 1) proposals for a regime governing the exploitation of Antarctic mineral wealth and 2) the potential end of the Treaty itself under the formula in Article XII, particularly in the face of opposition to the System from the Third World as demonstrated by recent activities of the UN.

For decades, Antarctica has been seen as a possible treasure trove of mineral wealth as it is geologically tied to both the vast resources of South Africa and the rich oil-fields off Australia's southern coast.[6] Only recently, though, has the exploitation of even part of this wealth become technologically feasible, and a great many engineering obstacles remain. Politically, this has meant the opening of negotiations on the establishment of a minerals regime for Antarctica. In so far as the records allow, the so-called "Beeby Draft", a working document for these discussions, will be examined as will the recent negotiations themselves (Chapter X).

Such negotiations come at an inconvenient time for the survival of the Treaty System in that the Antarctic agreements are coming under attack as a result of growing Third World doubts about the System. This is further compounded by the formula for ending the Treaty under Arcticle XII, by which the agreement may be radically altered by 1993 or dead by 1995. The demands for change from the Third World, coupled with the possible review of the Treaty, cast doubt upon the ability of the Antarctic Treaty System to survive in its present form into the twenty- first century. Although it is clearly too early to say how this doubt will be resolved, an examination of the activities of the UN *vis-à-vis* Antarctica will cast some light on the situation (Chapter XI).

In doing research into Antarctica Politics, the greatest obstacle is the secrecy in which the System is shrouded. Despite French and British efforts in the 1960s to declassify the records of Consultative Meetings,[7] the data have not been available publicly. Indeed, the history of the System recounted in this study is drawn from documents that seem to have slipped through the cracks.

In the United States, Antarctic policy is a matter for the Departments of State and Defense and the National Science Foundation (NSF). Memoranda and proposals are circulated by the Department of State to the other two organizations. Thus, copies of the American position papers and minutes of meetings can be found in the records of the NSF and US Navy as well as in the State Department files. Although the State Department is very diligent in keeping the papers locked away, the priorities of the Navy and of the NSF are different, and in their archives can be found a great many State Department records as well as an occasional foreign source. Although foreign corroboration is somewhat lacking (due to the Soviet Union's obsession with secrecy and Britain's 30-year rule to cite but two examples), enough exists in the American records to write some sort of history of the Antarctic System.

In the case of more contemporary information, the documents are part of active files and therefore, must be secured through other means. Here, the international environmentalist lobby has been particularly effective. By monitoring the Consultative Meetings and mineral negotiations from outside the conference room, they have obtained some data that is worthy of attention.

As mentioned earlier, the Antarctic Treaty System is unpopular in some quarters, such as the UN and the Organization of African Unity, and that unpopularity is due, in part, to the secrecy of the System. Although secrecy is clearly necessary in diplomacy, secrecy to the extent that it exists in Antarctic politics becomes detrimental to the System. Those who would wholeheartedly support the status quo are, by classification of records, denied the very facts they need to put their case forward intelligently in any debate on Antarctica. If any reform is needed in the Antarctic System, it is an opening of the record. Much of the hostility to the System would vanish when it can be shown that, despite some failures, the present arrangements are working. The only reason for maintaining secrecy is a fear that in opening the System to public scrutiny, there would be an undermining of the delicate negotiations in progress. While it is easy to sympathize with such an opinion, it appears to be an unfounded fear. In reading the history of the Antarctic Treaty System in the 1960s, it is obvious that any harm declassification would bring would be undetectable.

NOTES

[1]F. M. Auburn, *Antarctic Law and Politics*. (London: C. Hurst and Co., 1982), pp. 1-2.

[2]For a fuller examination of all the events of the first Consultative Meetings, see, Jeffrey D. Myhre, *The Antarctic Treaty Consultative Meetings, 1961-68: A Case Study in Cooperation, Compliance and Negotiation in the International System.* (PhD disseration: London School of Economics and Political Science, 1983).

[3]Article IX, paragraph 1 (f) of the Antarctic Treaty.

[4]The Agreed Measures for the Conservation of Antarctic Fauna and Flora, Recommendation III-VIII.

[5]Recommendation III-IX.

[6]The theory of plate techtonics holds that the continents of the planet were at one time joined in a super-continent called Gondwanaland. The present geography of Earth is

6

the result of continental drift, with the continents "floating" in different directions at a slow pace. Antarctica, when it was part of Gondwanaland, bordered South Africa and Australia. Thus, it is assumed, but unproven, that similar mineral deposits exist in Antarctica as have been found in South Africa and Australia. See, Philip W. Quigg, *A Pole Apart: The Emerging Issue of Antarctica.* (New York: McGraw-Hill Book Co., 1983), pp. 89-92.

[7]The efforts of the British, with French support, did not get beyond unsuccessful efforts at putting the matter on the agenda for the Fourth Consultative Meeting in Santiago. United States, Department of State, "Position Paper for the Fourth Consultative Meeting: Declassification of Official Records of the Antarctic Conference and Consultative Meetings." 1 June 1966, National Archives of the United States, Center for Polar Records, Record Group 307, Records of the National Science Foundation, Office of Antarctic Programs, Central Subject Files, Box 18, File 102D. Hereafter, such records will be cited only by Record Group (RG), box and file numbers.

CHAPTER II
TERRITORIAL SOVEREIGNTY IN ANTARCTICA[1]

One cannot hope to understand the politics of the Antarctic nor of the Antarctic Treaty System without a sound understanding of the central political question of the area, the issue of territorial sovereignty. If the claims to sovereignty that have been advanced are valid, then national jurisdiction is only submerged by the Treaty (See discussion of Article IV in Chapter IV). If such claims are not valid, then the allowances made for territorial claims are unnecessary. That, however, presupposes a clear decision on their validity and agreement among the Treaty Powers, and to a lesser extent the world community, on that point. Such is not the case. The allowances for claims and for the divergent positions taken by the various Treaty Powers on the matter are the direct result of disagreement and discord between the concerned nations and an unclear view as to the status of the claims.

The difference of opinion on the question of territorial sovereignty is chiefly due to a difference of experience of certain states. Some have long traditions of Antarctic involvement, while others are relative newcomers to the region. The varying histories tend to cause divisions. The unclear status of the claims is due to the condition of international legal principles; they are rather unclear on the matter. This is further compounded by differing views between the Treaty Powers as to what the law actually is. In order to comprehend these differences and the unclear status of the claims, it is necessary to see first how title to territory is acquired under modern international law, and then, briefly to examine each state's record of Antarctic exploration and research. This will not give a clear-cut answer to the question of territorial sovereignty, but it will show the difficulties the Treaty Powers had, and continue to have, as a result of these conflicting views.

Of the states involved, seven of them, maintain claims of territorial sovereignty over portions of the Antarctic (Argentina, Australia, Chile, France, New Zealand, Norway and the United Kingdom).[2] The other signatories to the Antarctic Treaty made no such claims, although some reserve the right to advance such claims in the future.[3] The question of acquiring territorial sovereignty is a legal one first and foremost, but one cannot ignore its underlying political thrust. States will base their claims on the prevailing principles of international law as much as they possibly can; in this way, they can muster a maximum amount of support for their claim as they are upholding law and the international order. This is the political side to international law, and the support the law-abiding state enjoys is political influence that can help ensure the acceptance of its claim by the world community. In short, it is good propaganda and good

8

politics to obey legal conventions when possible, or to give the appearance of doing so.

So, the discussion turns to the central issue of Antarctica, how can a state gain legal title to a territory? According to one leading jurist, there are five modes for obtaining title to territory under international law: 1) subjugation, i.e., a state may take territory from another by force of arms, 2) accretion, which means that the forces of nature work so as to change the geography of an area, 3) cession, whereby the title is transferred by provision of a treaty, 4) prescription, which is the transfer of title over time from one state to another, and 5) the occupation of heretofore unoccupied lands.[4] Given the uninhabited nature of the Antarctic continent prior to this century, it is obvious that the fifth mode, occupation, is the only one to have any bearing on the discussion here. In order to illustrate and explain what international law has to say regarding the matter of title by occupation, a review of three legal decisions will prove useful. Those cases are: 1) The Island of Palmas Case,[5] 2) The Clipperton Island Award[6] and 3) The Legal Status of Eastern Greenland Case.[7]

To begin with the Island of Palmas Case, the story is a short one. The Island of Palmas (also known as Miangas) is an island that is situated between the Philippines and what at the time were the Dutch East Indies, now the nation of Indonesia. Spain had claimed the island by right of discovery, and at the end of the Spanish-American War, Spain was forced to cede the Philippines and other territories to the United States. As demarcated in the peace treaty that ended the conflict, the Island of Palmas was part of the territory of the Philippines (The island's location at 5° 30' North and 127° East places it quite close to the Philippine island of Mindinao). In 1906, the United States learned that the Dutch considered the island to be part of their East Indies territories, basing their claim upon several treaties with local princes, which established the latter in a state of vassalage to the Netherlands. The result of the ensuing diplomatic exchange was an agreement to submit the matter to arbitration, having also agreed that Max Huber, a Swiss jurist, would act as sole arbitrator.[8]

The American case was based on America's acquisition of Spanish rights by the peace treaty, that is by cession. The Americans argued that Spain had acquired legal title by virtue of discovery in the sixteenth century. At that time, the American case went, discovery was adequate to give Spain title and that no change had occurred in that status until the cession in 1898. In addition, America claimed the island by virtue of its contiguity to the Philippine archipelago.[9]

In presenting the other side of the case, the Netherlands maintained that the island was theirs on the basis, not of discovery (they did not contest the point of Spanish discovery), but of exercise of state acts, either directly or through corporate agents of the Dutch government, as far back as 1677, perhaps even 1648. The Dutch cited several treaties from the seventeenth century onwards that established the sovereignty of the Netherlands over the disputed territory.[10]

In the end, Judge Huber found in favor of the Netherlands. He found that the Dutch had exercised sovereign rights as they had argued and that their title existed when Spain ceded the Philippines to America.[11] Thus, the Island of Palmas could not pass to America as part of the Philippines as it did not belong to Spain in 1898.

With regard to the American case, Huber admitted that title was granted by mere discovery at the time Spain found the island. However, he went on to say that without any act of sovereignty thereafter, the title would be of dubious quality. There was an "inter-termporal" international law that had to be observed, viz., the maintenance of sovereignty by exercise of rights and duties; the claim must be reaffirmed. Spain had obviously failed to do this, as the Dutch proved by their very presence on the island, and therefore, it could not be said that Spain had title at the time of the cession of territory to the United States.[12] As for the contiguity argument from the Americans, Huber rejected it, "The title of contiguity, understood as a basis of territorial sovereignty, has no foundation in international law."[13]

Thus, the decision in the Island of Palmas Case establishes, with a great deal of clarity, three points relevant to acquiring territory by occupation: 1) discovery alone is no longer (although it once was) a sufficient basis for a claim to territorial sovereignty; discovery does, however, establish an "inchoate title". That is, "... [discovery] does give rise to an exclusive right to occupy the area";[14] 2) related to discovery, there must be consolidation or actual displays of sovereignty before there is a title; and 3) contiguity is not a legitimate basis for a claim of sovereignty.

Moving on to the Clipperton Island Award, one finds that the facts in the case are a bit more intricate than those of the Island of Palmas Case. On 17 November 1858, a French naval officer took possession of the uninhabited island on behalf of France as per orders. Geographic details were noted, and some of the crew disembarked. The French left behind no sign of their sovereignty upon their departure. However, on 8 December 1858, the government of then-independent Hawaii was informed of the French claim, and a notice was published in a journal in Honolulu. In 1897, an American flag was raised on the island at the approach of a French ship. The French protested to the American government, and the United States denied any claim to the island. Between 1858 and 1897, there were no acts of French sovereignty.[15] Also in 1897, Mexico occupied the island claiming it by Spanish discovery, and as a successor state to the Vice-Royalty of Mexico, the United States of Mexico inherited Spanish rights under uti possidetis juris.[16] To settle the dispute, France and Mexico submitted the issue to arbitration by King Victor Emmanuel III of Italy.[17]

In his decision, Victor Emmanuel found for France. First of all, he held the Spanish discovery was unproven. Hence, he did not have to pronounce on the concept of uti possidetis juris, holding it to be irrelevant to the case. If Spain had no rights to the island, Mexico could not have succeeded to them upon the collapse of the Spanish empire. Second, Mexico had shown no intention to exercise any sovereignty rights prior to the occupation in 1897. Third, and highly relevant to the Antarctic situation, Victor Emmanuel held that France had fulfilled the requirement of effective occupation in so far as it was necessary given the uninhabited nature of the island. The trappings of sovereignty, e.g., currency, postal services, police forces, etc., are largely unnecessary in an unpopulated region. France showed an *animus occupandi*, the will to act as sovereign when necessary; this was demonstrated by its protest of the flag-raising incident to the United States. France had, therefore, not lost title through neglect, "[s]he never had the *animus* of abandoning the island, and the fact that she had not exercised her authority there in a positive manner does not imply the forfeiture of an acquisition already definitely perfected."[18] This is the point of greatest significance with regard to Antarctica. An *animus occupandi* must exist for a claim to be made, while sovereignty need only be expressed in so far as the situation of the territory, inhabited or not, requires. Sovereign acts are the manifestations of the *animus*, and sovereignty will be expressed in support of the *animus* as often as circumstances warrant to prove the existence of the will to act as sovereign.

As for the third legal decision, the Legal Status of Eastern Greenland Case, the facts are somewhat confusing and date back to the Middle Ages. Therefore, only the most important ones will be enumerated.[19]

Norway had originally colonized Greenland in the eleventh century, but these settlements had disappeared by the fifteenth century. Other attempts by Norway to colonize the territory occurred in the eighteenth century, but by 1776, Denmark had settled and established a trade monopoly there. Throughout the nineteenth and early twentieth centuries, the Danes settled the western part of Greenland. Also in this century, Denmark passed legislation for the administration of Greenland, and Denmark made reservations in treaties regarding Greenland that other powers had accepted. Norway, though, had not given up its interest in Greenland, having sent several expeditions there since 1889. In 1931, Norway announced its intention to occupy Eastern Greenland, and Denmark took the case to the Permanent Court of International Justice.[20]

The Danish case argued that Greenland came under Danish sovereignty because said sovereignty had been exercised continuously and over a long period of time. Denmark also cited treaties with Norway wherein the whole of Greenland was recognized as a Danish possession. In addition, the 1919 statement by a Norwegian minister to the effect that Norway would not impede recognition of Danish sovereignty over all of Greenland was also emphasized.[21]

From the Norwegian perspective, the area Norway had intended to occupy was *terra nullius*, belonging to no one, by virtue of the fact that Denmark had not made any occupation of the area. Also, the diplomatic efforts of the Danish government in 1915 and again in 1922 to gain recognition of Danish sovereignty over all of Greenland contradicted the claim to long occupation.[22]

In the decision, the court held that Denmark had sufficiently exercised sovereignty so that its control extended over all the island and not just the colonized areas. This was, in part, based on the relatively inaccessible nature of Greenland due to the severity of the climate. In any case, Norway's assertion was held to be untrue. As for the contradiction between the diplomatic offensives of 1915 and 1922 and the claim by Denmark to a long-established title, it was, in the majority opinion, irrelevant to the case.[23]

In synthesizing the results of these cases, one finds the law on title by occupation to be neither black nor white but an unsatisfying shade of grey. Discovery alone is not adequate as a basis for claiming territorial sovereignty; it must be followed by state acts and occupation. On the other hand, in cases where acts and occupation are unrealistic or impossible, the mere will to act as sovereign suffices. Therefore, it is possible to claim a nearby territory without actually administering it; however, any contiguity has no bearing on the claim under international law. If the reader is confused at this point, he will find himself in the company of many a good international lawyer.

> *The main legal problem with regard to occupation has been to define the degree and kind of possession effective to create a title and to define the area of territory to which such a possession might be said from time to time to apply.*[24]

One further point relevant to any discussion of international law and territorial sovereignty in Antarctica is the so-called "sector theory" or "sector principle", which is an attempt to define the area of territory to which title applies. Its validity under international law is suspect, at best,[25] but several states claim Antarctic territory using this idea as support. Indeed, the claims to Antarctic territory are usually referred to as "sectors", e.g., the French sector, or the Argentine sector.

Originally, the sector theory was meant to apply to the Arctic, not the Antarctic. It

> *... provides that when the territory of a state within the Arctic Circle, such as that of Canada [the country proposing the sector theory for the North Polar region], is contiguous to areas of ice or land that extend to the North Pole, and which are not possessed by another state, the right of sovereignty over the entire intervening space may in fact be asserted.*[26]

The manner in which the area is delineated is a neat piece of the cartographer's art. The meridians whereat the eastern-most and western-most points of a state's territory lie are extended to the Pole, where all longitude lines intersect. The wedge thus formed is then closed off in the south, in the case of the Arctic, by the state's northern coast.

Under international law as illustrated in the three legal cases earlier, it is apparent that the sector theory is without foundation. It ignores inchoate title based upon discovery and exploration, and it pays less attention to effective occupation.[27] At best, it is a claim by way of contiguity, which Judge Huber struck down in the Island of Palmas case. Moreover, it is not even customary law (law derived from state practice) because certain polar states, e.g., Norway, reject its validity.[28]

While it may be argued that the sector theory, despite its uncertain legality, addresses the Arctic situation well, the same may not be said of its application to the other end of the world. At Earth's northern end, there is an ocean, albeit ice quite often, surrounded by land, which establishes a convenient, if not altogether legal, baseline for the sectors. The Antarctic, though, is the negative image of the Arctic in more than name; it is a continent surrounded by an ocean. Thus, there is no "natural" baseline for Antarctic sectors. Moreover, if the Antarctic Circle were used as the boundary for sectors, as in the Arctic, no state would be entitled to put forth a claim as none lies south of the Antarctic Circle. If 50° South latitude were chosen as the relevant parallel, only Argentina and Chile would be eligible as claimants (and their sectors would be quite narrow). At the equator, scores of states could advance claims to their own sector, but this would still exclude France, Norway and the United Kingdom (states with claims to portions of Antarctica) as well as Belgium, Japan, Poland, the Soviet Union, the United States and West Germany (all Consultative Parties to the Antarctic Treaty).[29]

Despite the questionable value and legality of the sector principle in the Antarctic, six of the seven claimant powers use it in defense, in modified form, of "their" territories. With the exception of the British, Antarctic sectors have a baseline at 60° South; the British runs at 58° South between 50° West and 80° West and at 50° South between the remainder of its claim from 20° West to 50° West. Argentina's sector lies between 25° West and 74° West, and Chile's runs from 53° West to 90° West. (The over-lapping claims of Argentina, Britain and Chile are hotly disputed, and it has been argued cogently that this overlap was a factor in the South Atlantic War of 1982 involving Argentina and Britain.) New Zealand's claim covers 150° West to 160° East, France's from 142° East to 136° East, Australia's from 160° East to 45° East exclusive of the French sector.[30] The unclaimed territory from 90° West to 150° West is reserved for the United States by the claimant powers, but as yet, the Americans have not overtly accepted the territory.[31] Norway's claim will be discussed shortly, as it is not technically a sector.

The claims issue brings up the next major point, the postures and positions of the countries involved in Antarctica. As it is the territorial disposition of the Antarctic that fundamentally divides the states there, that division will be contained in the discussion beginning first with the claimant nations and then turning to the non-claimants.

CLAIMANT POWERS

Argentina: Argentina entered the Antarctic stage twice around the turn of the century, once to rescue a stranded Swedish expedition in 1903, and again at the invitation of the Scottish National Antarctic Expedition to take over a weather station in the South Orkneys in 1904. That particular station remained Argentina's only Antarctic outpost until after the Second World War.[32] Argentina's first territorial claim came in 1927 in a message to the Universal Postal Union, wherein Argentina included in its territory "... Polar lands not yet delimited."[33] In 1942, the ship, *Primero de Mayo*, took an expedition to the Antarctic Peninsula that left plaques declaring Argentina's claim to lands lying between 25° West and 68° 34' West with 60° South as West with 60° South as the baseline for the sector.[34] Bases on the peninsula have been manned by Argentina since 1947. In 1954, Argentina purchased an ice-breaker from West Germany, becoming the only country apart from the United States to have such a vessel for Antarctic uses.[35] In 1957, Argentina formally incorporated its sector into its metropolitan territory.[36]

Argentina's claim rests on four points, only one of which holds any water: 1) the succession to original Spanish rights, which is questionable since Spain's rights were none, having neither discovered, occupied nor exhibited any sort of *animus occupandi* on the continent; 2) geographical proximity, meaning contiguity, which has no validity in claiming territory and the 700-mile distance between Argentina and the Antarctic Peninsula makes proximity a loose term; 3) geological affinity, based on the idea that the Andes submerge at Tierra del Fuego to resurface in the south as the Antarctic Peninsula, a claim by contiguity muddled with doubtful geology; and 4) effective occupation of the South Orkney weather station since 1904, and subsequent bases, although this must certainly be insufficient to allow a claim of 45° in width.[37]

Chile: Although possessing a slight history of Antarctic interest prior to the Second World War, Chile did not truly take much interest in the Antarctic before 1940. Then, President Aguirre Cerda claimed a sector from 53° West to 90° West without a baseline.[38] In 1947, a permanent base was set up on Greenwich Island in the South Shetlands. The follow- ing year, the President opened the O'Higgins station personally. In 1956, the first tourist overflight of Antarctica was made by Chilean National Airlines. Additionally, in 1955 and 1956, administration of Chile's claim was taken from the Foreign Ministry and was placed under the Governor of Magallanes Province, thus incorporating the land into Chilean metropolitan territory.[39]

The basis of Chile's claim is identical to that of Argentina, and therefore, just as suspect. At best, Chile can claim effective occupation since 1947, but the claim over-laps both Britain's and Argentina's, and either of those may well have prior title. Be that as it may, both Chile and Argentina jealously protect what they consider to be their metropolitan territory in Antarctica, and suggestions of international controls are immediately rejected by both.[40]

Britain: To recite the history of British involvement in Antarctica would be a very long, and for the purposes at hand, an unnecessary task. Bearing that in mind, some of the highlights will suffice to clarify Britain's position in the Antarctic scheme of things. The British explorer, Captain James Cook, discovered the South Sandwich Islands as long ago as 1775. Edward Bransfield surveyed the South Shetland Islands in 1819- 20 and is believed to be the first, or one of the first, to record a sighting of the mainland. In the early twentieth century, Biscoe, Ross, Scott, Shackleton and

Weddell carried out extensive exploration. The Wilkins-Hearst Teams in 1928-30 were the first to use aircraft on the continent. Extensive mapping was carried out in the 1930s by several British expeditions. The Second World War required a temporary halt to British activity, but "Operation Tabarin" in 1943-45 was designed to re-assert a British Antarctic presence. Since the war, British operations have increased; for the International Geophysical Year (IGY), Britain operated no less than thirteen stations in the Antarctic and sub-Antarctic.[41]

Britain's claim, the first advanced for Antarctica, was made in 1908, but as that also claimed the tip of South America, this was refined in 1917. It extends from 20° West to 80° West with two baselines, at 50° South for the area from 20° West to 50° West, and 58° South for the remainder.[42] The claim is based on inchoate title acquired by virtue of discovery and exploration and the perfection of this title by effective occupation of its Antarctic bases and islands. Britain relies on the sector theory more to define the shape of its claim rather than as a basis for the claim itself.

The dispute between the South Americans and the British is one of the greatest potential problems that any state's Antarctic policy must face. Covering one-fifth of the continent, the disputed territory has been the focus of many diplomatic protests. The crisis of 1947-48 that threatened to turn into a shooting war fortunately led to an agreement between the rivals that no warships would be sent south of 60° South. Despite that, the South Atlantic War of 1982 demonstrates the degree to which each side is committed to preserving its rights in the area.

Australia: The Australian claim of 1933 was actually a British Order-in-Council claiming a vast sector, from 160° East to 45° East. Australians, though, carried out a good deal of exploration on their own; their first expedition came in 1911-14.[43] During the IGY, three bases were run by Australia; a fourth, handed over by the US in 1959, has been Australian since the end of the IGY.[44]

The Australian claim is relatively solid, based on effective occupation following acquisition of inchoate title conferred by discovery and exploration. It is weakened, though, by its vast size, covering 115° out of 360°; it is difficult to see how effective occupation to the entire area has been established despite Australia's bases. There is no doubt that the Australians have effectively occupied part of the continent but surely not thirty per cent of it. Nevertheless, Australia does seem to have exhibited an *animus occupandi* by rejecting the original calls for the internationalization of the continent.[45]

New Zealand: Like Australia, New Zealand's Antarctic Sector was originally a claim advanced by a British Order-in-Council, made in 1923. New Zealand did some exploring, e.g., the joint British-New Zealand expedition of 1929-31, but New Zealand has been a less-than-zealous claimant. Indeed, it was New Zealand that proposed the internationaliza- tion of Antarctica after the Second World War.[46] To some extent, this may be

said to weaken New Zealand's claim. In addition, New Zealand coope-
rates closely with the United States in logistical matters.[47]

France: The history of the French in the Antarctic displays a large gap in
the center. In the eighteenth century, French explorers discovered Bouvet
Island and the Kerguelen Archipelago. In the nineteenth century, 1837-40
to be precise, Captain d'Urville discovered Terre Adelie on the mainland.
Then, the gap appears, and it persists until 1924 when the French officially
claimed Terre Adelie, a small sector between 136° East and 142° East. After
the war, the French operated a pair of stations and have sent several expeditions to the Antarctic.[48]

The French claim, in one sense, is perhaps the most defensible of all
Antarctic claims in that it is the smallest. Moreover, the effective occupation that followed discovery of Terre Adelie is enhanced by an agreement
in the first part of this century between the Commonwealth and France.
Essentially, it was a simple agreement to allow for mutual over-flight of
territories, but its effect was mutually to recognize Antarctic claims.[49] The
French have opposed any internationalization of the continent, not
surprising with their strong claim, but the French favor close scientific
cooperation and regulation.[50]

Norway: At the beginning of Antarctic exploration, Norwegians were
sought out, as were other Scandinavians, by expeditions because of their
vast practical experience in the Arctic. In addition, Norwegian whaling
interests brought whaling ships from Norway to Antarctic waters as early
as 1892.[51] The icing on the cake of Antarctic exploration, the distinction of
being the first to the South Pole, went to Norway's Roald Amundsen in
1911. In 1939 in response to German encroachment into territory only
explored by Norwegians, Norway claimed the coast of Antarctica from 20°
West to 45° East. Many huts and bases were established, but only one was
open and used in the IGY.[52]

Norway is unique among the claimant states in that the Norwegians
reject the sector theory without reservation, chiefly in response to their
interests in the Arctic. For whatever reasons, they claim only the coastal
area which they have mapped and occupied. Although a claim to the
South Pole could have been advanced after Amundsen's expedition, no
such claim has been made. It is certain that the Norwegian claim is
strong, perhaps even stronger than the French; there is no boundary
dispute, their occupation has been effective, they have avoided claiming
vast areas at great distances from their bases, and they do not rely on the
sector theory at all. It is not surprising, therefore, that Norway has been
luke-warm to proposals for internationalization of Antarctica.[53]

Having outlined the positions of the claimants, the examination turns
to those states that have no claims to Antarctic territory.

NON-CLAIMANT STATES

Belgium: The Belgians were granted a place at the Washington Conference that produced the Antarctic Treaty based largely on the legacy of the "Belgica" expedition led by Baron De Gerlache in 1897-99. The importance of this effort rests in the fact that this was the first expedition to spend the winter, or "winter-over", in Antarctica.[54] In 1956, a base was established in the Norwegian claim. In 1960-61, the station was closed due to financial problems in the Belgian program. Belgium has since been almost uninvolved in Antarctica.[55]

Japan: An expedition led by Lieutenant Choku Shirase in 1911 marked the beginning of Japanese involvement in Antarctica, exploring the Ross Ice Shelf. In 1934, Japanese whaling vessels became a more or less permanent feature of the Southern Ocean. Japan made no claim of territorial sovereignty based on the explorations of the 1911-12 expeditions, and by the terms of the Peace Treaty of 1952, Japan renounced its territorial rights everywhere including the right to advance an Antarctic claim.[56] Japanese activities since the war have been chiefly scientific and due to continued whaling, partly commercial in nature.[57]

South Africa: Interest in the Antarctic by South Africa stems from proximity, as South Africa possesses two sub-Antarctic islands, Prince Edward and Marion. In addition, strategic concerns, given the political geography of the area, must contribute to this interest. In 1960, South Africa took over the operations of what is now Sanae station in the Norwegian claim. South Africa seems to be chiefly interested in scientific pursuits,[58] as there is little evidence of any other activity.

Soviet Union: Sailing under the flag of Tsar Alexander I, Admiral Bellingshausen circumnavigated the continent in 1819-21. During this voyage, the Soviets claim that he discovered the mainland, although this is disputed (it is possible that Bransfield of Britain or Palmer of America discovered it in 1820).[59] No other action was taken by Imperial Russia, nor did the Soviet regime act until it protested the Norwegian claim in 1939. The next time the Soviets were involved in Antarctica was with a whaling fleet in 1946.[60] In 1950, the Soviets informed the US and six claimants, excluding Chile, that it demanded a voice in the "final" resolution of the Antarctic question. The Soviets in the 1960s and thereafter, established many bases all over the continent, ignoring claims it refuses to recognize. However, in 1958 and 1959, the Soviet Union reserved its rights based on the explorations of Russians/Soviets. Soviet interest extends to the resources of Antarctica as well as the territory itself. Oil and gas, metals and fishing have all been prominent among Soviet declarations of economic interest. The Soviets pioneered the trawling of krill, a small crustacean found in abundance in the Southern Ocean, in 1961, thus adding that to its list of interests.[61]

United States: The full account of US involvement is better discussed in conjunction with the 1948 diplomatic events. Briefly, though, the US has been active in the Antarctic since 1820 starting with sealing and whaling. In this century, the expeditions of Byrd, Ellsworth and Finn Ronne have kept American involvement and interest alive. After the Second World War, the US used the Antarctic for military training operations and launched the biggest expedition of all time, Operation Highjump. No claim has ever been openly advanced, but the US has made its right to make a claim in the future quite clear.[62]

These states were the original twelve signatories to the Antarctic Treaty, and consequentally, the most important actors in the evolution of the Antarctic Treaty System. However, as provided for in Article IX paragraph 2 of the Treaty, other states have come to play a part in the Consultative Meetings. To date six countries have joined the Consultative club, and their actions become of interest in examining the negotiations for an Antarctic minerals regime (see Chapter X). Those new Consultative Powers are:

Poland: Poland received Consultative status after the opening of its base, Arctowski, in 1979. Like the Soviet Union, Poland has an interest in the exploitation of krill, and therefore, its interests are both scientific and economic.[63]

West Germany: As a successor state to the Third Reich, and because there is no peace treaty with Germany to forbid it, the Federal Republic could claim the rights acquired when Richter was sent to Antarctica by Hitler in 1939, which spurred the Norwegian Claim. Swastikas on steel shafts were dropped from aircraft as claim markers.[64] Given the interest in the Antarctic that Germany has shown in acceding to the Treaty,[65] this claim may come into play at a later date if the present System runs into difficulties. For now, however, science is the chief interest of the West Germans who received Consultative status in 1981.[66]

Brazil, India, People's Republic of China, and Uruguay: These four countries became the newest members of the Consultative club. Brazil and India received that status in 1983, just in time for the fourth special meeting on establishing a minerals regime for Antarctica.[67] The Chinese and Uruguayans joined the ranks of the Consultative Powers in 1985.[68] As they are such recent members, their impact on the System has yet to be felt. However, their very participation in Antarctic politics means a change in the nature of those politics. Apart from Chile and Argentina, there has been no Third World participation in Antarctic negotiations, and even in the case of those two, as claimants, their interests are different from the rest of the Third World's. Although it is too soon to judge what their influence means to the System, it does bode well for the future. Because of their participation, the Antarctic Consultative Meetings look less like gatherings of rich nations huddled together in secret to keep someting out of the hands of the less developed states. In short, these newcomers offer a wider range of views within the System.

ACCEDING STATES

As of 1985, there were also fourteen states have acceded to the Treaty but have not received Consultative status, that is, they support the agreement, while not fully participating in the Consultative Meetings. While their influence in the System is small, they are a part of it, and from their ranks will come the next Consultative Powers. They are: Bulgaria, Cuba, Czechoslovakia, Finland, East Germany, Hungary, the Netherlands, Papua New Guinea, Denmark, Peru, Italy, Rumania, Spain and Sweden.[69]

NOTES

[1]Part of this chapter is derived from Jeffrey D. Myhre, "Title to the Falklands-Malvinas Islands under International Law," *Millennium: Journal of International Studies.* (Vol. 12, No. 1, Spring 1983), pp. 25-38.

[2]John Hanessian, Jr., "National Activities and Interests in Antarctica. Part II: The Claimant Nations," *Polar Area Studies.* (Vol. 2, No. 6).

[3]*Ibid.*, "National Activities and Interests in Antarctica. Part III: The Non-Claimant Nations." (Vol. 2, No. 7).

[4]R. Y. Jennings, *The Acquisition of Territory in International Law.* (Manchester: Manchester University Press, 1963), pp. 6-7.

[5]*United Nations Reports of International Arbitrations and Awards, Vol. 2.* Permanent Court of Arbitration, 1928, US v. the Netherlands.

[6]*United Nations Reports of International Arbitrations and Awards, Vol. 2, 1932,* France v. Mexico.

[7]Permanent Court of International Justice. Ser. A/B 53,3, Denmark v. Norway, 1933.

[8]Wolfgang G. Friedman, Oliver J. Lissitzyn, and Richard Crawford Pugh (eds.), *Cases and Materials on International Law.* (St. Paul, Minnesota: West Publishing Company, 1969), p. 440.

[9]Arnold McNair and H. Lauterpacht, *Annual Digest of Public International Law Cases: 1927-28.* (London: Longmans, Green and Company, 1931), Case no. 1.

[10]*Ibid.*, Case no. 68.

[11]*Ibid.*, Case no. 1.

[12]*Ibid.*

[13]W. Friedman, O. Lissitzyn, and R. C. Pugh, *Cases and Materials ...*, p. 448. For a similar case see "The Miniqiers and Ecrehos Case" *International Court of Justice Reports.* (1953).

[14]John Hanesian, Jr., *Polar Area Studies*. (Vol. 2, No. 5), p. 11.

[15]W. Friedman, O. Lissitzyn, and R. C. Pugh, *Cases and Materials* ..., p. 449.

[16]H. Lauterpacht, *Annual Digest of Public International Law Cases: 1931-32.* (London: Longmans, Green and Company, 1935), Case no. 50.

[17]John Hanessian, Jr., *Polar Area Studies*. (Vol. 2, No. 5), p. 10.

[18]*American Journal of International Law*. (Vol. 26, 1932), p. 394.

[19]A full account of this can be found in PCIJ Ser. A/B no. 53. 5 April 1933.

[20]H. Lauterpacht, *Annual Digest* ... *1931-32.* Case no. 49.

[21]W. Friedman, O. Lissitzyn, and R. C. Pugh, *Cases and Materials* ..., *passim*.

[22]*Ibid*.

[23]Concurring and dissenting opinions differed with this view. See PCIJ Ser A/B no. 53, pp. 96 and 102.

[24]R. Y. Jennings, *Acquisition of Territory* ..., p. 20.

[25]Howard J. Taubenfeld, "A Treaty for Antarctica," *International Conciliation.* (Jan. 1961), pp. 249-255.

[26]John Hanessian, Jr., *Polar Area Studies*. (Vol. 2, No. 5), p. 12.

[27]*Ibid.*, p. 13.

[28]F. M. Auburn, *Antarctic Law and Politics.*, p. 29.

[29]*Ibid.*, p. 24.

[30]Philip C. Jessup and Howard J. Taubenfeld, *Control for Outer Space and the Antarctic Analogy.* (New York: Columbia University Press, 1959), map insert.

[31]F. M. Auburn, *Antarctic Law and Politics*, p. 75.

[32]John Hanessian, Jr., *Polar Area Studies*. (Vol. 2, No. 6), p. 3.

[33]Carlos Aramayo Alzerreca, *História de la Antártida.* (Buenos Aires: Editorial Hemisferio, 1949), p. 162.

[34]This was later extended to 74° West. Robert D. Hayton, "The 'American' Antarctic," *American Journal of International Law.* (Vol. 50, July 1956), p. 590.

[35]John Hanessian, Jr., *Polar Area Studies*. (Vol. 2, No. 6), p. 7.

[36]*Ibid.*

[37]*Ibid.*

[38]Robert D. Hayton, "The 'American' Antarctic," p. 586.

[39]F. M. Auburn, *Antarctic Law and Politics*, p. 49.

[40]For the South American perspective, see Armando Braun Menendez, *Pequeña História Antártica*. (Buenos Aires: Editorial Francisco de Aquirre, S. A., 1974).

[41]John Hanessian, Jr., *Polar Area Studies*. (Vol. 2, No. 5), p. 4.

[42]Philip C. Jessup and Howard J. Taubenfeld, ... *Antarctic Analogy*, map.

[43]G. C. L. Bertram, "Antarctic Prospect," *International Affairs*. (Vol. 33, No. 2, April 1957), p. 148.

[44]John Hanessian, Jr., *Polar Area Studies*. (Vol. 2, No. 6), p. 11.

[45]*Ibid.*

[46]For the definitive works on New Zealand and the Antarctic, see F. M. Auburn, *The Ross Dependency*. (The Hague: Martinus Nijhoff, 1972) and L. B. Quartermain, *New Zealand and the Antarctic*. (Wellington: New Zealand Government Printers, 1971).

[47]John Hanessian, Jr., *Polar Area Studies*. (Vol. 2, No. 6), p. 11.

[48]*Ibid.*

[49]*Ibid.*

[50]W. Sullivan, *Quest for a Continent*. (New York: McGraw Hill Book Company, 1957), *passim*.

[51]John Hanessian, Jr., *Polar Area Studies*. (Vol. 2, No. 6), p. 4.

[52]G. C. L. Bertram, "Antarctic Prospects," p. 150.

[53]Robert D. Hayton, "The Antarctic Settlement of 1959," *American Journal of International Law*. (Vol. 54, 1960), p. 350.

[54]F. M. Auburn, *Antarctic Law and Politics*, p. 4.

[55]G. C. L. Bertram, "Antarctic Prospect," p. 149.

[56]John Hanessian, Jr., *Polar Area Studies*. (Vol. 3, No. 1).

[57]F. M. Auburn, *Antarctic Law and Politics*, p. 205.

[58]Robert D. Hayton, "Antarctic Settlement ...", p. 349.

[59]F. M. Auburn, *Antarctic Law and Politics*, p. 78.

[60]*Ibid.*, pp. 78-80.

[61]Many other states have been involved in krill harvesting, e.g. Brazil, Spain and Sweden, but the Soviet Union's efforts are the most far-reaching.

[62]See Chapter III for more on the Americans' activities.

[63]F. M. Auburn, *Antarctic Law and Politics*, p. xvi.

[64]Christof Friedrich, *Germany's Antarctic Claim: Secret Nazi Polar Expeditions.* (Toronto: Samisdat Publishers, Ltd., 1978), *passim*. And John Hanessian, Jr., *Polar Area Studies.* (Vol. 2, No. 7), p. 21.

[65]F. M. Auburn, *Antarctic Law and Politics*, pp. 116-117.

[66]Philip W. Quigg, *A Pole Apart...* , p. 149.

[67]For Brazil, see F. M. Auburn, *Antarctic Law and Politics*, pp. 59-60. India was a long-standing critic of the Treaty. See "India Establishes Foothold in Antarctica," *Washington Post*, 2 February 1983, p. A16. Also, Eco (Vol. XXVI, No. 1, January 18-27, 1984), p. 1.

[68]Greenpeace International, "The Future of the Antarctic: Background for a Third UN Debate," 25 November 1985, p. 4.

[69]*Ibid.*, p. 5.

CHAPTER III
ORIGINS OF THE ANTARCTIC TREATY, 1948-1959

The Antarctic Treaty of 1959 is a most remarkable agreement. At the height of the Cold War, the Treaty bound the US and USSR to demilitarization of the entire continent, to ban nuclear testing in the region, and to allow on-site inspection of their respective facilities. At the same time, it bound Argentina, Britain and Chile to ignoring, to freezing their overlapping territorial claims. Additionally, it required all signatories to exchange all scientific data gathered in Antarctica.

Often the Treaty's origins are traced to the International Geophysical Year (IGY). According to records recently released by the United States' Department of State, the Treaty was really spawned by an American State Department facing a possible war between its allies and lacking a policy with which to address the problem. This predicament, however, can only be understood by briefly retracing American exploration of Antarctica and by examining what the State Department did regarding those expeditions.

American involvement in the Antarctic dates from the late eighteenth and early nineteenth centuries when US citizens and ships played a prominent role in whaling in Antarctic waters. Indeed, one of the candidates for the title of discoverer of the Antarctic mainland was an American whaling captain, Palmer of the *Hero*.[1] Charles Wilkes, with Congressional funding, explored the coast of Antarctica from 1838-1842.[2] The twentieth century expeditions of Admiral Richard Byrd and of Lincoln Ellsworth continued this interest.

Had the Antarctic remained the exclusive preserve of gentlemen adventurers, there would be very little to say about Antarctica of a nonscientific nature. In the event, though, the British issued the first territorial claim over part of Antarctica in 1908,[3] bringing politics to the seventh continent. As mentioned in the previous chapter, several other states (Argentina, Australia, Chile, France, New Zealand and Norway) followed with claims of their own, occasionally advancing conflicting claims.

In the case of the United States, however, there are no official claims, nor is there any recognition of territorial claims advanced by other states. Unofficially, though, the story is quite a different one. The privately-financed Byrd expeditions of 1929-31 and 1933-35, as well as those by others, e.g., Lincoln Ellsworth's 1935-36 expedition, advanced claims to explored territory on behalf of the US.[4] It is quite comprehensible that explorers should leave claims and markers thereof behind; it would be embarrassing to have one's government advance a claim without some on-the-spot proof of the claim (as France found in the case of Clipperton Island). The reason why the United States government has not taken up these claims, claims made on its behalf by its own citizens, is less obvious.

In 1924, five years before Admiral Byrd's first expedition, then-Secretary of State Hughes unveiled official thinking in what is now known as the Hughes Doctrine.

> ... [D]iscovery of lands unknown to civilization, even when coupled with the formal taking of possession, does not support a valid claim of sovereignty unless the discovery is followed by an actual settlement of the discovered country.[5]

Although roughly noting the distinction between an inchoate and a perfected title, the Hughes Doctrine has received largely justified criticism on a number of counts. First and most damning of all, it seemed to justify a lack of an Antarctic policy by the US during the 1920s and 1930s.[6] Also, the Hughes Doctrine raised the criteria for advancing a claim to territorial sovereignty, thereby upsetting claims by other states without giving any advantage to the United States.[7] Although the Hughes Doctrine was, in actuality, merely a Department of State's interpretation of contemporary international law, as opposed to a statement of policy, it was bad politics. Worse, it remained official thinking for the next fifteen years. During that time, and despite the decision in the Legal Status of Eastern Greenland Case (particularly the point that the climate and its effect must be considered when the degree of effective occupation needed for a claim is in question), the only action taken by the State Department *vis-à-vis* Antarctica was to assist Byrd's efforts in exempting supplies for his 1929-31 expedition from customs duties in New Zealand.[8] It may have been useful to Byrd's efforts, but it was hardly a policy.

In 1939, though, a proposed expedition to Antarctica sparked a review of policy and of the Hughes Doctrine. It concluded that Hughes had not given adequate consideration to the issue of climate and therefore, had over-emphasized the degree of occupation required to perfect title. This review essentially incorporated the Denmark v. Norway case into American thinking six years after the court's ruling. That said, the planned expedition was to establish two permanent bases on the continent just to be sure.[9]

After the interruption of exploration caused by the Second World War, the states with a tradition of interest in Antarctica returned to the continent.[10] America was no exception and in the period immediately following the war, the US staged enormous exercises, Operation Highjump in 1947 and Operation Windmill in 1947-48.

To this day, Operation Highjump remains the largest single effort ever undertaken in Antarctica. Originally, it was intended to be a US Navy training exercise in the Arctic. In order to be less provocative to the Soviets, the Antarctic was chosen as the site for the exercise. The entire maneuver, if it can be described as such, involved 4,700 men, 13 US Navy ships (including an ice-breaker and an aircraft-carrier) and 11 members of the press.[11] In all 70,000 photographs were taken of approximately 350,000 square miles of land, including roughly 60% of the Antarctic coast. Of that vast territory, 25% is presumed to have been unseen prior to High- jump. Operation Windmill, while important, was a smaller, follow-up expedition that failed to equal the glamour of Highjump: Metro-Goldwyn-Meyer released a documentary of Highjump entitled *The Secret Land*.[12]

In policy terms, Highjump (and by extension Windmill that followed it) had a five-fold purpose. First, there was the obvious plan of training personnel and testing equipment in conditions of extreme cold. Second, the work of previous expeditions, in particular that of the United States Antarctic Service Expedition, was to be continued and furthered. A third motive behind Highjump and Windmill was the experience to be gained in logistical techniques for establishing polar bases. Fourth, there was a genuine desire to conduct scientific research. A fifth objective, kept secret until the operation was declassified in 1955, was to establish the strongest possible basis for a territorial claim to as much of the continent as possible.[13]

At first glance, this would appear to be a complete reversal of America's pre-war position, of the Hughes Doctrine. Yet that position did not reject territorial claims outright. It merely required a high degree of effective occupation to perfect inchoate title acquired by discovery. As Operations Highjump and Windmill proved, the state of technology in the late 1940s was more than adequate to establish effective occupation even under Hughes' terms. Therefore, America was in a position to settle in Antarctica and advance a claim without contradicting the Hughes Doctrine; a legal tangle was overcome. So, it was perhaps no surprise that the State Department announced in 1947 that an American claim was on the way.[14]

What, then, became of the proposed American claim? Bluntly, it was legally possible, but politically foolish, to advance a claim in the late 1940s. At the time of Highjump, Windmill, and Finn Ronne's private expedition, the territorial dispute between Britain and the South American claimants threatened to become a war. Diplomatic protests began as early as 1946.

In all, the events of 1946-48 started with sabre-rattling, apparently for domestic consumption in Argentina. On 3 June 1946, Argentina demanded to know the extent of the British Antarctic claim and declared to the Universal Postal Union that letters carrying the British-issued Falkland Islands Dependencies stamps would be treated as letters lacking postage. In 1947, both Argentina and Chile established bases on islands claimed by Britain, and the dispute intensified.[15]

On 15 August 1947, the Rio Treaty was signed by several New World states, including the US, Argentina and Chile, to provide for the common defense. The area affected by the pact extended, at Argentine insistence, to the South Pole between 24° West and 90° West. This covers the Argentine and Chilean claims entirely and all disputed territory in Antarctica. Although the US made a reservation to the effect that the agreement did not affect the sovereignty of the area defended,[16] if shots were fired over Antarctic claims, western solidarity in the newly-born Cold War would be among the first casualties.

In December 1947, the British frigate *HMS Snipe* was dispatched to the Southern Ocean. On 23 January 1948, Argentina announced that it would be sending troops to Antarctica. In mid-February of the same year, the cruiser *HMS Nigeria* was ordered to join the *Snipe*.[17]

At about this time, faced with a foreshadowing of the 1982 South Atlantic War, the United States began a policy study to resolve the Antarctic question. The US government documents of the period show that the State Department sought advice from the Department of the Interior and the Pentagon's Joint Chiefs of Staff.

The Department of the Interior justified its interest in the issue of Antarctica by citing its general interest and concerns with natural resources. Secretary of the Interior Krug proposed that, from his Department's point of view, a special trusteeship with common control would be the best solution. Such a system would have to provide adequate measures for the conservation of natural resources and the environment. In addition, it would have to ensure that the United States received a "fair" share of the resources. Additionally, Krug urged the Department of State to advance a territorial claim as soon as possible.[18] On the one hand, he called for internationalization of the Antarctic and on the other, a division of territory.

Quite obviously, the interest of the Joint Chiefs of Staff (JCS) in the matter was strategic. The JCS held that in 1948 Antarctica had no strategic value at all. Mineral discoveries or the establishment of military bases by other powers (which Argentina had threatened to do) could alter the assessment the JCS had made. Due to the continent's geographic location, forming the southern limit of Drake's Passage, access to it would have to be denied to potentially hostile states, and that must be done in such a way so as not to prejudice American interests in the Arctic, which was much more significant in strategic terms. Pursuant to this, the JCS argued that the United States should only relinquish its right to press a territorial claim if Antarctica could be shown to have no strategic value in the future. The defense establishment was opposed to any suggestion of a UN Trusteeship because it would leave possible enemies in a position to interfere with Antarctic matters. A condominium was more acceptable to the JCS but that too had to exclude potentially hostile powers, and it should not prejudice the situation in the Arctic. Last, it would not be in the interests of the country, according to the Joint Chiefs, to demilitarize Antarctica. The final recommendation was to pursue an American claim and to adjudicate the territorial disputes that would be caused.[19]

Inter-agency discussions continued throughout May of 1948. Then on 9 June, the Policy Planning Staff issued a policy paper, PPS-31, originally classified "secret".[20] This study is important for two reasons; first, it is the first real Antarctic policy America pursued, and second, many of its concepts are now part of the Antarctic Treaty and Approved Recommendations of the Consultative Meetings.

As set forth at the very beginning of PPS-31, American Antarctic policy sought to eliminate international disputes over territory, to preserve the area for scientific uses, and to protect US national interests. The last vague term seems directed at strategic and economic concerns with special attention being paid to the Soviet Union.

The Policy Planning Staff made several salient points with regard to the territorial issue. First was the reiteration of the no-claims principle; the US made no claim to Antarctic territory and recognized none advanced by other states while reserving the right to advance a claim at some future date. This remains part of US policy in the 1980s.[21] Second was the acknowledgement of the South American-British dispute, and third, a related point, was the Rio Treaty and its role in the dispute. Fourth and last, there was support for the Joint Chiefs position that control of Antarctica was not vital to the security of the US.

On points of economic consideration, the document was pessimistic. Mineral wealth was excluded from the realm of commercial probability, due to the thickness of the ice on the continent (measured in miles in places) and the problems that that brought. Living resources, mainly whales, were being exploited by factory ships. Therefore, land bases for processing of catches were unnecessary. In short, any economic value regarding the Antarctic mainland or islands was regarded as negligible at most.

For scientific interests, PPS-31 observed that America's past expeditions, whether privately or publicly funded, had been chiefly of a scientific nature. Meteorology was singled out for special consideration, the observation being made that in any solution to the Antarctic question would require the inclusion of various sub-Antarctic islands for the purpose of gathering weather information.

The centerpiece of PPS-31 was the strategic issue. Although the US did not need to control Antarctic territory to safeguard its own security, access to the continent and the surrounding islands had to be denied to potential enemies, especially the Soviet Union. Further, the divisions in the western camp over Antarctica were of benefit to Moscow. Most worrisome of all to the Americans was the possibility that the Soviets might send an expedition to the area between 90° West and 150° West, the very area to which America had the strongest claim and the only unclaimed portion of Antarctica. The only positive strategic interest the United States had was to use Antarctica as a cold-weather training area for its armed forces.

Based on those enumerated interests and concerns, PPS-31 made several recommendations. Reduced to their barest content, these recommendations entailed the advancing of an American claim, properly timed, so as to exclude the Soviets from the unclaimed sector and so as to put America on an equal footing with the claimant powers. Also, the US should press for a UN trusteeship for Antarctica or some similar form of internationalization.[22]

Attached to PPS-31 was a draft agreement on Antarctica. This proposal, although in significant ways different from the Antarctic Treaty of 1959, laid the foundations for the present Antarctic System. It provided for the area south of 60° South to become a special UN trusteeship. The eight claimants (the US presumably having advanced a claim of its own prior to reaching any accord) were to be designated as the administering authority, this authority to be jointly exercised. The claims issue was to be settled not by the renunciation of claims but by the merging of them all.[23]

This approach promised to avoid the difficulties involved in adjudicating the South American-British dispute and those disputes likely to arise from an American claim. Each state was to share sovereignty over the whole of the area concerned. While strictly speaking, sovereignty of states is indivisible and, therefore, probably cannot be shared, merged claims would solve more problems that it would create.

Although the Antarctic was to be a UN Trusteeship, administration of the region would remain in the hands of the Eight, as the joint administering authority. To coordinate policy, a Commission was envisaged with a Secretariat to carry out the appropriate functions. The Commission was to be the liaison between the administering states, the UN specialized agencies and the relevant, non-UN international bodies. At the same time, one of the Eight was to be a member of the UN Trusteeship Council.[24]

In particular, the Commission was directed to establish a scientific organization that would plan scientific efforts in Antarctica. States would also present to this body their scientific and economic development plans for Antarctica. These plans would then go to the Commission for approval to ensure their consistency with the Agreement.[25]

Other measures included an undertaking on the part of the signatories to ensure peace and security of the region. There was no intention to demilitarize the Antarctic. The area could, and presumably would, be defended by the military of the Eight, all of whom were members of the western bloc.[26]

These proposals were passed to the British government on 25 June 1948. The response was not unreceptive, but the British echoed the Joint Chiefs' suspicion of Soviet meddling if the continent were made a UN Trusteeship. Additionally, the intent of the concept of trusteeship and the conditions of Antarctica differed so much that the British feared that the US proposal would distort the concept of a trusteeship for "inhabited and backward territories."[27]

With the British critique in hand, the US redrafted the proposal. The changes made were of no substance save that the trusteeship idea was dropped in favor of an eight-state, multiple condominium. The Commission would exercise full legislative and executive authority. It had instructions to cooperate with the UN and relevant international organizations, but what shape the cooperation was to take was not made explicit.[28]

On 9 August 1948, the revised draft was circulated among the seven claimant states. Reaction ranged from acceptance by Britain of the draft as a basis for discussion and favorable interest on the part of New Zealand, to Norwegian indifference, Chilean negativity and Argentine hostility.[29]

As this discussion was taking place, the State Department was planning the extent of the American claim. Samuel W. Boggs, then the State Department's Geographic Adviser, delineated a potential claim. It would include the entire territory from 35° West to 180° to 13° East with the following limitations:

1) From 35° to 135° between 68° [South] and 81° [South], all the mainland and islands explored or mapped by US expeditions and all areas encompassed therein mapped solely by US expeditions, except for areas of the Palmer Peninsula and adjacent islands seen or mapped by non-Americans;

2) From 135° to 140° East, all lands seen by US expeditions, save for the South Pole area where Norway's claim by virtue of Roald Amundsen's 1911 expedition is recognized and coastal areas seen and mapped by non-Americans;

3) Between 140°E and 13°E, all areas north of 75° [South] mapped by US expeditions excluding coastal areas mapped by other nations.[30]

This claim can be seen in a number of ways. Legally, it is contentious. While the US has never accepted an Antarctic sector theory, whereby states claim territory never seen by their nationals, some states do. The Boggs claim ignores sectors completely, leaving a great deal of room for adjudication. On the other hand, it may be justified if the sector principle is as unfounded in international law as most jurists say, because it accepts prior expeditions as bases for contrary, superior claims. Politically, it was a fine example of the carrot and the stick. It is obvious that the US preferred an international settlement to a division of the continent. So, on the one hand, the proposed claim would upset the established sectors and create so many disputes that division would become possible only after long, slow adjudication, which several states had already refused. If need be, the US could paralyze, or at least threaten to paralyze, the division of the continent. On the other hand, it provided bargaining counters for any negotiations on an international solution. If claims were to be merged, it would make the conflicts arising from Boggs' proposal irrelevent, but no one could guarantee that that would be the formula for solving the problem of territoriality. A claim of this magnitue, one may argue, would force the claimant governments to the bargaining table.

That is not to say that the claim demarcated by Boggs was not without its dangers. In upsetting the established sectors, the US would be handing the Soviets a golden opportunity for mischief-making. Exactly how much Soviet "meddling" was occurring in 1948 is debatable. The perception in Washington, though, was that any chance for Soviet inter- ference had to be eliminated. If the Americans were concerned about the advantages the Soviet Union could acquire from the Latin American- British dispute, how much worse would the position be if America became a disputant as well as a claimant state?

By October 1948, the initiative to create a multiple condominium was clearly out of steam.[31] From the responses received, the American goal seemed to be overly ambitious. As the South Americans held the Antarctic question to be one of national sovereignty,[32] clearly a multiple condominium was beyond hope.

In phoenix-like fashion, however, the Chilean rejection contained the seeds of a new initiative. Chile proposed an agreement for the exchange of scientific data coupled with a moratorium on territorial issues for at least five years. While bases and expeditions would operate as usual under the Chilean proposal, the signatory powers would renounce these actions during the given period as a basis for asserting or supporting a territorial claim.[33]

This idea seized the attention of several members of the State Department. Scientific cooperation, a matter on which all Antarctic powers could agree in principle, would be a beginning. Some still hesitated because of the moratorium on claims, but this position eventually gave way.[34] In an undated document, the *modus vivendi*, as the Chileans had dubbed the idea, was proposed by the Department of State to the National Security Council.[35] The proposals in PPS-31 were recognized as the dead issues they had become, and a modified version of Chile's proposal was advanced. This *modus vivendi* provided for eight things: 1) a declaration by the Eight of their desire to avoid conflict in Antarctica, 2) agreement that a solution to the territorial question would be sought, 3) a freeze on all claims for five to ten years, 4) free movement of all scientific teams over all of Antarctica, 5) full exchange of all scientific data acquired, 6) a scientific coordinating commission would be created, 7) cooperation for the advancement of common interests and protection of common rights, and 8) formal consideration of an Antarctic conference before the expiration of the *modus vivendi* agreement.[36]

This initiative never got off the ground, due in part to the Korean War and in part to the slow discussions between America and Chile on the drafting of an agreement. As late as 1951, Washington and Santiago were trying to formulate a proposal.[37] In 1950, though, the possibility of an eight-power accord vanished with a Soviet note to the US and six claimant states (no note was sent to Chile because diplomatic relations between Chile and the USSR had been served) that demanded that the Soviets be included in any Antarctic settlement.[38] Despite this, it is interesting to note how much the Antarctic System owes to the 1948-49 initiatives.

Under the 1959 agreement, freedom of scientific work and the exchange of data and personnel (Articles II and III) are taken from the *modus vivendi* idea. The freezing of claims (Article IV) is also derived from that. The boundary of the treaty area (Article VI) is part of the PPS-31 draft agreement. The limitation on the number of participating governments (Consultative status under Article IX) is clearly part of PPS-31. Of all the matters of substance in the 1959 Treaty, perhaps only demilitarization of Antarctica (Article I) has its origin later than 1949. Even then, such demilitarization denies any potential enemies of the United States military access to Antarctica, a goal dating from 1948. In other ways separate from the actual Treaty, parts of the present System date in concept from the 1948-49 events. Loosely, the Consultative Meetings themselves serve the same role as the Commission in the condominium proposal. Under that draft agreement, the Comission would set up a scientific body to coordinate research. While the Scientific Committee on Antarctic Research was not established by the Consultative Powers, SCAR does serve the same technical support role envisioned by this proposal.

While the Soviet note of 1950 altered the nature of Antarctic politics, the biggest change began that same year at a dinner party in Silver Spring, Maryland. On 5 April, Dr. James Van Allen hosted a gathering of scientists, and many of the guests discussed the need for a coordinated, international effort similar to the First and Second Polar Years. Interest was so great that some of Van Allen's guests took the idea to the International Council of Scientific Unions (ICSU), a roof organization for the major scientific bodies. Thus the International Geophysical Year was conceived.[39]

The International Geophysical Year (IGY) has been the subject of a good portion of the literature on the Antarctic and justly so. To expand on that particular body of work would be unnecessary,[40] but to omit the IGY would be impossible because the IGY is so closely linked to the Antarctic Treaty of 1959.[41]

By 1952, the ICSU had established a special committee to help coordinate plans for what was then seen only as the Third Polar Year in 1957-58. Due to requests from the world scientific community in 1952, though, the plan was expanded to cover not just the poles, but the whole world. ICSU, in 1953, created the *Comité Spécial de l' Année Géophysique Internationale* (CSAGI). The CSAGI was to coordinate the national IGY committees who were to submit their scientific plans in May 1954.[42]

First and foremost, the IGY was a scientific event. However, it had its political side as well. In 1954, the US revived the idea of an Antarctic claim,[43] but for fear of upsetting the work of the independent, nongovernmental Special Committee on Antarctic Research (SCAR) in coordinating IGY efforts in Antarctica, the idea was shelved. In 1956, the Soviets established their first base, Mirny, in Antarctica in preparation for the IGY.[44] Without the IGY, one can easily imagine how loud western protests at this would have been, particularly those from Australia which claims the territory in which Mirny was placed. In the same year, India's call for UN control of Antarctica was suspended for the duration of the IGY.[45]

Although to have ended 31 December 1958, the IGY was extended another year to 31 December 1959, under the name of International Geophysical Cooperation-1959 (IGC). IGC extended the scientific programs underway to allow a fuller, more complete collection of data. In Antarctica, this also meant the extension of the gentlemen's agreement on claims; no actions during the IGC (as with the IGY) would be taken as a basis for asserting, supporting or refuting a territorial claim. Politically, this was fortunate. As early as March 1957, Australia was having second thoughts about the proximity of the Soviets both to the Australian mainland and Australia's claim. There was even speculation in the Australian

32

press that Mirny would be converted to a submarine base after the end of the IGY.[46] Fears in other countries also existed over what would happen with the expiration of the IGY/IGC. On 2 May 1958, the US began informal talks in Washington to consider the issue of Antarctica's future beyond the IGY. These talks continued until well past 31 December 1958, and had the IGC not come along to buy time for the diplomats, Antarctica would be open to the same sort of tensions that existed in 1948 on an even greater scale. Thanks to the extension, the talks had time to progress, and they were successful enough for the US to issue an invitation to those states in Antarctica for the IGY to attend an Antarctic Conference on 15 October 1959.[47] On 1 December, the Antarctic Treaty was signed.

NOTES

[1]Kenneth J. Bertand, *Americans in Antarctica, 1775-1948.* (New York: American Geographical Society, 1971), p. 72.

[2]Philip Quigg, *A Pole Apart ...*, p. 13.

[3]*Polar Record.* (Vol. 5, No. 35), pp. 241-43.

[4]M. M. Whiteman, *Digest on International Law, Vol. II.* (Washington, DC: Government Printing Office, 1963), p. 1245.

[5]Letter to A. W. Prescott in G. H. Hackworth, *Digest of International Law, Vol. I.* (Washington, DC: Government Printing Office, 1940), p. 399.

[6]B. M. Plott, *The Development of United States Antarctic Policy.* (PhD thesis: Fletcher School of Law and Diplomacy, Tufts University, 1969), pp. 25, 76-7. It is unfortunate that this particular study has not been published as it does an excellent job in extracting American official thinking from the rather sparse record.

[7]F. M. Auburn, *Antarctic Law and Politics*, p. 2.

[8]B. M. Plott, *Development of US Antarctic Policy*, pp. 31-2.

[9]United States, Department of State, *Foreign Relations of the United States, 1939, Vol. 2.* (Washington, DC: Government Printing Office, 1956), p. 10.

[10]It must be remembered that non-belligerent Argentina and Chile were active in Antarctica during the war.

[11]B. M. Plott, *Development of US Antarctic Policy*, p. 116.

[12]*Ibid.*, p. 115.

[13]Walter Sullivan, "Antarctica in a Two-Power World," *Foreign Affairs.* (October 1957), p. 174.

[14]"US Maps Formal Claims," *New York Times*, 6 January 1957, p. 21.

[15]B. M. Plott, *Development of US Antarctic Policy*, pp. 120-22.

[16]United States, Department of State, *Conference on Antarctica*. (Washington, DC: Government Printing Office, 1960), pp. 8-9.

[17]B. M. Plott, *Development of US Antarctic Policy*, pp. 127-9.

[18]United States, Department of State, *Foreign Relations of the United States, 1948, Vol. 1, part 2*. (Congressional Information Service, 1980, H920.5), *passim*.

[19]*Ibid.*

[20]*Ibid.*, pp. 977-87. PPS-31 was also circulated as National Security Council Paper 21 of 18 July 1948.

[21]Interview with R. Tucker Scully, Director of the Office of Oceans and Polar Affairs, United States Department of State. 10 February 1983.

[22]*Foreign Relations ... 1948, Vol. 1, part 2*, pp. 982-2.

[23]Articles I-III "Draft Agreement on Antarctica," *Ibid.*, p. 985.

[24]*Ibid.*, Articles IV and V, pp. 985-6.

[25]*Ibid.*, Article VI.

[26]*Ibid.*, Article VII.

[27]*Foreign Relations ... 1948, Vol. I, part 3*, p. 992.

[28]*Ibid.*, pp. 997-1000.

[29]United States, Department of State, *Foreign Relations of the United States, 1949, Vol. I*. (Congressional Information Service, 1980, H920.10), pp. 800-1.

[30]*Ibid.*, p. 1001.

[31]*Ibid.*, p. 1001-2.

[32]*Ibid.*

[33]*Ibid.*, pp. 806-7.

[34]*Ibid.*

[35]*Ibid.*, pp. 806-9. This particular document was undated, but most likely it was written between May and September of 1949.

34

36Ibid., pp. 807-9.

37United States, Department of State, *Foreign Relations of the United States, 1951, Vol. I.* (Congressional Information Service, 1980, H920.26), pp. 1734-6.

38The text of the Soviet note is appended to Peter A. Toma, "The Soviet Attitude toward the Acquisition of Territorial Soveteignty in Antarctica," *American Journal of International Law.* (Vol. 50, July 1956), pp. 611-26.

39Frank J. Ross, Jr., *Partners in Science: The Story of the International Geophysical Year.* (New York: Lothrop, Lee and Shepard Company, Inc., 1960), p. 13.

40See Walter Sullivan, *Assault on the Unknown: The International Geophysical Year.* (New York: McGraw Hill Book Company, 1961).

41Article II of the Treaty notes the IGY by name, demonstrating the close ties between the two.

42Walter Sullivan, *Assault on the Unknown ...*, p. 27.

43National Security Council Memorandum 5127, July 1964. Cited in F. M. Auburn, *Antarctic Law and Politics*, p. 75.

44F. M. Auburn, *Antarctic Law and Politics*, p. 79.

45Walter Sullivan, *Assault on the Unknown ...*, p. 414.

46"Russian Base in the Antarctic: Australian Concern," *The Times* (London), 7 February 1957, p. 7.

47For a slightly more detailed examination of the 1957-1959 period, see Philip Quigg, *A Pole Apart ...*, pp. 142-47.

CHAPTER IV
THE ANTARTIC TREATY AND
CONSULTATIVE MEETINGS UNDER ARTICLE IX

The Antarctic Treaty of 1959 has been evaluated in a number of ways. At the time of American ratification of the agreement, Senator Engle decried it as a betrayal of American interests and as a triumph for the Soviet Union.[1] Others see it as a temporary solution to the Antarctic question, the best possible accord in 1959 but not the definite answer to the problem.[2] Still others claim it established a rich nations' club designed to deny poorer countries their "rights" in Antarctica.[3]

However one judges the Treaty, one cannot dispute that its provisions achieved the four American objectives desired at the outset of the Washington Conference: 1) the preservation of Antarctica for peaceful purposes, 2) the establishment of freedom of scientific activity in the region, 3) the decreasing of political tensions and 4) the establishment of a system of consultations between the interested states.[4] To understand how this was achieved and how the Treaty's provisions influenced the first Consultative Meetings, a discussion of the Treaty article-by-article will prove useful.[5]

In Article I, the signatories agreed to the first American aim, that "Antarctica shall be used for peaceful purposes only."[6] Often this Article is said to have demilitarized the continent, but in actuality, Antarctica was never militarized. That unique and happy situation is preserved by the complete banning of military installations, weapons tests and military maneuvers. This blanket banning is, however, not as absolute as it appears. In paragraph 2, it is specified that military personnel acting in a capacity other than a military one is permissible. This provision merely acknowledges that the logistical problems endemic in supporting any Antarctic activity are often best solved by military administration. Many, if not most, of the first Antarctic expeditions were military ones. In the particular case of the United States, the Navy has been the organization responsible for support activities from the outset.

With "demilitarization" agreed, scientific activities are addressed in Article II. In essence, the signatories agreed under this Article to extend the cooperation begun during the IGY/IGC. This is far from remarkable, and there appears to have been little, if any, disagreement over this.[7]

Article III elaborates on scientific freedoms and duties of the signatories. The Treaty provides for advance notice of plans, the exchange of personnel between bases and expeditions, and the exchange of scientific data gathered in the Antarctic. Further, cooperatioin between the contracting parties and UN and non-UN international organizations is pledged.

Perhaps the most important feature of the Treaty is Article IV. Essentially, this extended the gentlemen's agreement on Antarctic claims from the IGY. Claims are frozen by the terms of Article IV. This almost certainly was not every nation's first choice as a solution to the problem of sovereignty because it is no solution at all. It puts off solving the claims issue until the expiration of the Treaty. It is a fairly unsatisfying compromise from any perspective. However, the wide divisions between the participants in the Washington Conference made any other outcome impossible. On the one extreme, New Zealand was prepared to renounce title to its sector in favor of an international regime, ideally under the auspices of the UN.[8] At the other end of the spectrum, Chile made it clear that it could not accept any form of internationalization; "the Chilean Antarctic territory does not have the character of a colonial possession but is part of its metropolitan territory and forms part of its southernmost province."[9] Echoing this, Argentina maintained that the Washington Conference was not "... convened to institute regimes or to create structures."[10] With such divisions, the Treaty was unable to alter the *status quo* and was forced to support it by default.

Under Article V, the Contracting Parties made Antarctica the world's first nuclear weapon-free zone. Although nuclear power was not prohibited (for a time America's McMurdo base had a fission reactor), the detonation of bombs and the storage of waste from nuclear reactors in Antarctica were banned entirely. There was some inconvenience as a result of this provision, such as necessitating the shipment of wastes from the McMurdo reactor to the United States for storage. On the whole, however, it is consistent with the terms and spirit of Articles I-III. It supports the idea of peaceful uses of Antarctica and reduces the danger of contaminating the environment, the outdoor laboratory.

Deceptively short and seemingly routine, Article VI defines the area of application of the Treaty. All provisions of the Treaty apply to the area south of 60° South, including ice shelves. A great many problems for international lawyers have arisen over the further provision that no part of the Treaty affects the freedom of the high seas.[11] Primarily, there is the question of exactly what the high seas are near Antarctica. If the territorial claims that have been advanced possess any validity, then there is a territorial sea contiguous to the coast. If on the other hand, there is no sovereignty over Antarctica, there can be no territorial sea, and the high seas begin at the coast. The entire issue turns on whether there is a sovereignty in the region, and this issue was shelved under the terms of Article IV.[12] As a result of this ambiguity, there is little discussion of the freedom of the high seas except in very abstract terms.

Article VII is a diplomatic milestone, equally as significant as Article IV. This was the first instance in history, and to date the only one, in which the United States and the Soviet Union agreed to on-site inspection of their respective installations. "Observers" are allowed free access at all times to stations, ships and aircraft. The practicality of such an inspection is less than the reading of Article VII suggests, though. A surprise inspection is simply impossible in the Antarctic; one does not just "drop-in" on an Antarctic station. In the face of the most severe climate in the world, advance warning is essential as a safety precaution, so any violation of the terms of the Treaty can be covered. Such inspections are a rarity in any case (perhaps the personnel have better things to do than check up on one another), and no violation of the Treaty has ever been revealed by such inspections.[13]

Under Article VIII, the powers tried to allow for something resembling law and order in Antarctica. Observers, exchanged scientific personnel and members of their staffs are under the jurisdiction of the state that designated them observers or sent them on the exchange. Thus, a Chilean observer inspecting a South African installation is under Chilean jurisdiction. The difficulty in dealing with the question of jurisdiction is, of course, that it is directly related to, indeed part of, territorial sovereignty. One of the rights and duties of a sovereign state is the exercise of criminal jurisdiction within its territory. The case of a hypothetical observer committing a crime in the claim or at an installation of a state other than his own does not present a real problem because of Article VIII. State A yields the right to exercise criminal jurisdiction (assuming for the sake of argument that is has any such right) to State B which sent the observer; it is an instance not unlike diplomatic immunity. However, not all such cases would be covered by the terms of Article VIII.

> *Imagine a French tourist who arrives at the US McMurdo station on board a Norwegian ship on a tour arranged by a British agency and is the victim of a crime committed by a person of unknown nationality in the New Zealand sector.*[14]

No mention of such a confusing situation exists in Article VIII. It is, therefore, fortunate that those in Antarctica to date have been less inclined to criminal activity than the general population and have given rise to no such case.

Skipping over Article IX for now, which will be taken up in detail later, Article X binds the signatories to ensure that no one disobeys the intent of the Treaty. In the case of one's own citizens, this is easily done. With regard to non-citizens, subjects of other states, difficulties arise. Legally, questions abound as to whether a claimant could take any action against such a person while remaining within the intent of Article IV, or whether any action could be taken against citizens or governments of non-signatory countries.[15] Politically, the only question is would a signatory act against a state that is not party to the Treaty? Largely, that would depend on the gravity of the offense. Littering may not be pursued, but the establishment of a military base certainly would be. Moreover, in any situation pitting Treaty Powers against outsiders to the System, one can expect that the signatories would close ranks in preservation of the System.

Article XI provides for the settlements of disputes that arise. Typical of the zealously guarded autonomy some nations desire in Antarctica, no binding arbitration or any similar mechanism is required. It appears that those states that have consistently resisted any diminution of their control over Antarctic policy resisted the inclusion of mandatory arbitra- tion in the Treaty. The operative clause in Article XI merely calls for the peaceful resolution of disputes.

Article XII covers amendments and the termination of the Treaty. Under paragraph 1 section A, the Contracting Powers may amend the Treaty by unanimous agreement. This amendment enters into force as each state ratifies it; that is, it applies to the US as soon as the US ratifies it, while it does not go into effect for Argentina until Argentina ratifies it. Under section B of paragraph 1, any state that fails to ratify the amendment within two years is considered to have withdrawn from the Treaty. This fact is often overlooked in academic writings. The Antarctic Treaty could break down in just two years' time. If by failure to ratify an amendment, a claimant state withdrew, it could endeavor to restrict the actions of other states in its claimed territory, militarize its claim, use it for the storage of nuclear waste and so forth. This situation would return Antarctica to the 1940s. It is equally conceivable that a non-claimant could upset the balance by its withdrawal; it could advance claims, test nuclear weapons and so on. It is important to note that the Treaty has never been amended; apparently, each state involved realizes the potential an amendment carries.

Under paragraph 2 of Article XII, a different avenue for the termination of the Treaty is explained. Section A provides for a review conference thirty years after the Treaty entered into force, that is, in 1991, if any Consultative Power desires it. At such a conference, the Treaty can be amended by majority agreement (an important departure from the unanimity principle that pervades the Antarctic System) of all Contracting Parties (see *infra* for the distinction between a Contracting Party and a Consultative Party), under section B. These amendments enter into force upon ratification, just as do amendments under paragraph 1. Section C contains the termination formula; if an amendment made at the review conference is not ratified by all Contracting Parties within two years, states may give notice of withdrawal from the Treaty effective two years beyond that. Thus, since a review conference could be held as early as 1991, but no earlier, amendments from that meeting would have to be ratified no later than 1993. Therefore, a state could not withdraw from the Treaty until two years later, 1995. In those intervening years, negotiations would have time to save the System from total collapse. By the same token, the termination of the agreement is more likely under this formula than under the one in the preceding paragraph. Under paragraph 1, a govern- ment would have to accept an amendment (due to the unanimity rule) and then refuse to ratify it. It would have to be almost deliberate sabotage. Under paragraph 2, a government that found itself in the minority on a proposed amendment would either have to change its position and ratify an amendment it opposes, or reject the change and open up the possibility of withdrawals from the Treaty. Although one would expect the various governments to have more political sense than to put a signatory in such a position, the danger remains.

Article XIII is generally a house-keeping provision. The Treaty is left open to accession by member states of the UN and other unanimously approved countries. The US government is declared the depositary government, is instructed to inform the various states concerned about ratifications, and is instructed to register the Treaty with the UN. Entry into force of the Treaty is upon ratification or accession as appropriate.

Article XIV declares Russian, French, Spanish and English to be the official, equally valid languages of the Antarctic Treaty. Seemingly innocuous, the problems this can cause in finding suitable wording in four languages with a common interpretation are obvious. In this, the Antarctic System is not unique; language is a problem for all international agreements.

Returning to Article IX, this provides for the machinery of the Antarctic System, and it is by way of this provision that the machinery, such as it is, evolved. According to Article XIII, paragraph 1, all UN members and other approved states may accede to the Treaty. Any state signing or acceding to the Treaty is a Contracting Party. However, the meetings held under the terms of Article IX are open only to Consultative Powers, which initially meant the original twelve signatories. These meetings were intended to deal with issues that would further the intent of the Treaty including: a) use of Antarctica for peaceful purposes only; b) facilitation of scientific research in Antarctica; c) facilitation of international scientific cooperation in Antarctica; d) facilitation of the exercise of the rights of inspection provided for in Article VII of the Treaty; e) questions relating to the exercise of jurisdiction in Antarctica; and f) preservation and conservation of living resources in Antarctica.

Paragraph 2 of Article IX allows for the expansion of the number of states entitled to attend Consultative Meetings (although only the original twelve could attend the first); acceding states must prove that they have sufficient interest to participate by conducting "substantial scientific research activity." Thus, there are two tiers to the Antarctic Treaty. The first is that of Contracting status: any member of the UN or any unanimously approved state may acquire this by depositing an instrument of accession with the US government. In the case of a state not in the UN, whose approval must be unanimous? That of the second tier, that of the Consultative Powers. The twelve participants of the Washington Conference gave themselves, and only themselves, the right to attend Consultative Meetings without reservation. Any other state must conduct enough research, by establishing a base or sending an expedition, to convince all twelve that it is entitled to join them at the Consultative Meetings.

This is the sheep-and-goats paragraph that translated means: Everyone is welcome and encouraged to accede to the treaty, but only the original twelve will participate in making decisions...[16]

These decisions also include who else may participate in making decisions. To date, only six nations, Poland in 1979, West Germany in 1981, Brazil and India in 1983, and Uruguay and the People's Republic of

China in 1985, have been given Consultative Status.[17]

It may be argued that in addition to the division between Contracting and Consultative Powers there is a split within the ranks of the Consultative Parties. The orginal signatories are entitled to attend Consultative Meetings by paragraph 1, "Representatives of the Contracting parties named in the preamble to the present Treaty shall meet ... ." Others are granted such status by virtue of demonstrated interest, meaning scientific research, under paragraph 2, but only "during such time as that Contracting Party demonstrates its interest in Antarctica ... ." Thus, the orginal Consultative Powers have that status as part of the Treaty's terms and can, therefore, only lose it by amendment to the Treaty. As this requires unanimity, at least until 1991, one of the original Consultative Powers can only lose its rights as a Consultative Power with its own consent. Poland, West Germany, Brazil, India, Uruguay and China are not Consultative Powers by virtue of the Treaty itself, but instead possess it because the other, orginial Consultative Powers have seen fit to grant it to them. A careful reading of Article IX paragraph 2 reveals that they can be stripped of this status. Should any of this second group of states cease its research activity, paragraph 2 would cease to apply, and it would lose its right to attend Consultative Meetings. Thus the orginal twelve Consultative Powers possess that status independent of their research activity, but all other states must continue research or forfeit Consultative Status.[18]

As for paragraphs 3,4, and 5 of Article IX, they confine themselves to the functioning of the Consultative Meetings and to the rights of Consultative status. Under paragraph 3, reports of inspections are to be circulated to all Consultative Powers. Paragraph 4 states that measures agreed to at the Consultative Meetings require unanimous approval by all Consultative Powers. Under paragraph 5, states may exercise any rights granted by the Treaty with or without facilitating measures having been agreed, meaning that the Meetings did not have the right to prevent acts permitted under the Treaty, only to make arrangements to ease the exercise of those rights.

Obvious from this review of the Treaty's contents, the Consultative Meetings are the main channel of negotiations for Antarctica. The Recommendations, those measure agreed to at the Meetings, are the arrangements that reconcile the problems encountered in Antarctica with the Treaty. They update and support the Treaty and prevent it from becoming out-dated and useless. Since the Antarctic System lacks a secretariat, the Consultative Meetings are the sole forum for "administering" the Antarctic, the sole prop of the System itself.

The main issues discussed at the first five Consultative Meetings will be examined in later chapters, but the myth of secrecy about Consultative Meetings is so pervasive that no real discussion of how they function exists. This comes as something of a surprise because the Rules of Procedure have been in the public domain since the Final Report of the First Consultative Meeting was published. Although scholars are obviously aware of them,[19] none ever thought them worth discussing, perhaps because how a matter is discussed loses importance if one does not know

that the matter actually is. While not absolutely necessary to understanding the evolution of the Antarctic Treaty System, the gap that exists in the
literature serves no purpose. Additionally, the rules governing debate can
sometimes influence the debate.

First of all, there are the rules concerning delegations. Delegations to
the Antarctic Treaty Consultative Meetings[20] consist of one Representative of each Consultative Power and whatever alternates, advisers and
staff are required. The names of these people are sent to the host government and other Consultative Powers before the Meeting.[21] The delegations' order of precedence follows alphabetical order in the language of the
host nation.[22] At the first session of the Meetings, delegations choose the
Chairman, customarily this is the Representative of the Host government who is elected by acclamation. All other Representatives serve as
Vice-Chairmen. Plenary sessions are usually presided over by the Chairman, but in his absence, the Vice-Chairmen take over according to the
order of precedence.[23] Secretarial duties are performed by a Secretary, who
is appointed by the Chairman subject to the approval of all the delegations.[24]

Next are the rules concerning the work of the Meeting. The opening
session of the Meeting is held in public, but all others are private unless
the delegations decide otherwise.[25] The Meeting is allowed to form
committees to carry out various functions and defines what is germane
for each committee so formed.[26] These committees are bound by the Meeting's Rules of Procedure in so far as they are applicable.[27] Either the
Meeting as a whole or committees thereof can form whatever working
groups necessary to undertake the business at hand.[28]

The next set of Rules of Procedure are those pertaining to the conduct
of business, the parliamentary procedure of the Meeting. A quorum of an
Antarctic Treaty Consultative Meeting is two-thirds of the Representatives at the Meeting.[29] The Chairman's powers and duties are to enforce
the Rules of Procedure, maintain order and to moderate proceedings as is
customary at international gatherings subject to the approval of all delegations.[30] No Representative may speak without the Chair's recognition,
which is granted on a first come first served basis. The Chairman may call
a speaker to order if he should go beyond the Rules of Procedure.[31] Any
Representative may raise a point of order, which the Chair must decide
immediately. Should the Representative be dissatisfied, he may appeal to
the Meeting, and the Chair may be over-ruled by a majority of those
present and voting. This point of order may not, however, touch on a
matter of substance, solely on a matter of procedure.[32] The Meeting may
place limits on the amount of time allowed to a speaker and the number
of times a Representative may speak.[33] At any time during a discussion, a
Representative may ask for an adjournment of the debate. This is decided
by a majority vote that follows two Representatives speaking for and two
against the adjournment. The time allowed for these speeches may be
limited by the Chairman subject to the approval of the delegations.[34] Also
at any time, a Representative can move a closure of debate on an issue. A
motion to close debate is handled identically, but no one may speak for

such a motion (two speeches may be made against it still), but this rule does not apply in committees.[35] The difference between these similar motions is that adjournment is only a break in the debate, which may be taken up later. Closure of debate is an end to all debate on a topic. In the case of suspending or adjourning the Meeting, there is an immediate vote without debate.[36] The order of precedence of those motions is: 1) motion to suspend the Meeting, 2) motion to adjourn Meeting, 3) motion to adjourn debate, and 4) motion to close debate.[37] Voting on matters of procedure is decided on a one delegation-one vote basis with a simple majority deciding the issue.[38]

Although English, French, Spanish and Russian are the official languages of the Antarctic Treaty and its Consultative Meetings,[39] a speaker may address the Meeting in any language so long a translation into one of the official languages is provided by the speaker's delegation.[40] Recommendations of Consultative Meetings, which have the status of executive agreements, must be approved by all Representatives of the Meeting and must be written into the Final Report.[41] The Final Report, which can also include a brief account of the proceedings, must be approved by a majority of Representatives and is then given to the Secretary, who in turn, transmits it to the various governments for their consideration.[42]

Finally, the Rules of Procedure can be amended by a two-thirds majority vote of all Representatives participating in the Meeting. This, however, does not apply to Rule 23, concerning the approval of Recommendations. Amendment of Rule 23 requires approval by all delegations participating at the Meeting.[43]

Although a bit dry to all but the most avid parliamentarians, the Rules of Procedure demonstrate two things about the conduct of Meetings. First, the Chairman is under the tight control of the delegations. He may limit the time given to debates only with the approval of majority of delegations; he may have his rulings challenged by any Representative by a direct appeal to the Meeting. This is not unusual, neither in international nor national meetings, but it does underline the essentially decentralized nature of the System and the Meetings. Second, the unanimity rule pervades all substantive discussions. On matters of procedure, the simple majority is the most practical way of addressing disputes. Substantively, there is no room for dissent. The only place where substantive issues may be decided by a majority vote is in approving the Final Report, and there, the contentious issues are the Recommendations, which have already received unanimous approval.

Before embarking on a discussion of the main issues that the System faces, a word or two should be said about the arrangements for the Consultative Meetings. As mandated in Article IX, the First Consultative Meeting was held in Canberra two months after the Treaty entered into force, July 1961. The Second Consultative Meeting occurred a year later in Buenos Aires. This was followed by the Third in Brussels in June 1964, the Fourth in Santiago in November 1966 and the Fifth, in Paris in November 1968. Such Meetings continue to be held more or less regularly, but these first five are important in that they settled the course for the evolution of the Antarctic System. Until such time as the records of the other Meetings come to light, these also represent the only Meetings about which very much is known.

In diplomacy, preparation is every bit as important as the conference itself. In Antarctic politics, the Canberra and Buenos Aires Meetings were prepared at "interim meetings" held in Washington, and little is known about them. The Third Consultative Meeting was the result of nine "Preparatory Meetings" held in Brussels, and the record here offers a great deal of insight into the workings of the Preparatory Meetings. For the Santiago Meeting, a single, extended Preparatory Meeting was held. This idea seems to have been regarded as a failure, because the Paris Meeting's preparation occurred in a series of six Preparatory Meetings held in the French capital.

NOTES

[1] United States, Congress, *Congressional Record*, 8 August 1960, p. 15981.

[2] Philip Quigg, *A Pole Apart...*, p. 153.

[3] "India Establishing Foothold in Antarctica," *Washington Post*, 2 February 1983.

[4] B. M. Plott, *Development of US Antarctic Policy*, p. 197.

[5] For the full text of the Antarctic Treaty, see Appendix A.

[6] Article I, paragraph 1 of the Treaty.

[7] Philip Quigg, *A Pole Apart...*, p. 147.

[8] *Conference on Antarctica*, pp. 10-11.

[9] *Ibid.*, pp. 17-18.

[10] *Ibid.*, p. 31.

[11] See *infra* concerning the Agreed Measures for the Conservation of Antarctic Fauna and Flora.

[12] F.M. Auburn, *Antarctic Law and Politics*, p. 134.

[13] Philip Quigg, *A Pole Apart...*, p. 147.

[14] *Ibid.*, p. 151.

[15] See F.M. Auburn, *Antarctic Law and Politics*, pp. 184-204, for a more detailed examination of jurisdictional problems in Antarctica.

[16]Philip Quigg, *A Pole Apart...*, p.149.

[17]*Ibid.*

[18]Belgian research, to cite the most obvious example, has been intermittent as best, lending support to this interpretation of paragraph 2 of Article IX.

[19]F.M. Auburn, *Antarctic Law and Politics*, p. 156.

[20]The name is prescribed under the Rules of Procedure, Rule 1.

[21]Rules of Procedure, Rule 2.

[22]Rules of Procedure, Rule 3.

[23]Rules of Procedure, Rule 5. Under Rule 4, the Representative of the host country acts as temporary Chair until the election of the official Chairman.

[24]Rules of Procedure, Rule 6.

[25]Rules of Procedure, Rule 7.

[26]Rules of Procedure, Rule 8.

[27]Rules of Procedure, Rule 9.

[28]Rules of Procedure, Rule 10.

[29]Rules of Procedure, Rule 11.

[30]Rules of Procedure, Rule 12.

[31]Rules of Procedure, Rule 13.

[32]Rules of Procedure, Rule 14.

[33]Rules of Procedure, Rule 15.

[34]Rules of Procedure, Rule 16.

[35]Rules of Procedure, Rule 17.

[36]Rules of Procedure, Rule 18.

[37]Rules of Procedure, Rule 19.

[38]Rules of Procedure, Rule 20.

[39]Rules of Procedure, Rule 21.

[40]Rules of Procedure, Rule 22.

[41]Rules of Procedure, Rule 23, also Article IX, paragraph 4.

[42]Rules of Procedure, Rule 24. There seems to have been no attempt recorded to alter the Rules of Procedure.

[43]Rules of Procedure, Rule 25. The Rules of Procedure can be found in any and all of the Final Reports of Antarctic Treaty Consultative Meetings along with the Recommendations issued by each Meeting. These Final Reports contain virtually no record of what went on at the meetings, but rather list the results.

CHAPTER V
CONSERVATION

As mandated in Article IX, paragraph, 1 section F, one of the express purposes of the Consultative Meetings is to arrange for the protection of Antarctic wildlife. It should come as no surprise, then, that the issue of conservation was on the agenda of the Consultative Powers from the beginning. However, a commitment in principle to conservation is not the same as creating structures and mechanisms that can actually perform the function of protecting the biosphere.

Of particular significance in the conservation of the South Polar region is the nature of the environment itself. Because of the harshness of the climate, the usual fragility of an ecosystem is exaggerated. The severe cold requires special adaptations of the flora and fauna, and specialization becomes disadvantageous to an organism if the environment changes. For example, the tiny crustacean, krill, makes up the first link in the Antarctic food chain, and there is no adequate replacement for it. Thus over-harvesting of krill, or pollution of the sea could undermine the entire Antarctic food chain.

As Antarctica is a special case, one other point should be noted. In most environments, the introduction of human activity alters the environment radically, and humans must choose between their own interests and conservation. In Antarctica, the chief human activity is scientific research, and therefore, it is in the interests of humans, particularly biologists, that the introduction of *homo sapiens* does not affect the indigenous species. So long as science is the primary industry of the seventh continent, the protection of the Antarctic ecology is of benefit to humans. The debate in the present is whether this will, or should, continue. However, in the early years of the Treaty System, there was no doubt as to the need for conservation in the Antarctic. The negotiations were not concerned with whether there would be protection for the indigenous species, but rather, what form that protection would take.

In the case of conservation, the initial discussions in Canberra were hampered by the suddenness of the Meeting. As provided in the Treaty, this Meeting was set for two months after the agreement entered into force. This resulted in somewhat hurried preparation of positions and occasionally in needlessly long debates.[1]

When the First Consultative Meeting turned its attention to the entire question of conservation, the British took the lead in proposing that a recently passed resolution of SCAR be adopted as a Recommendation. This resolution, among other things, called for the recognition of Antarctica as a "nature reserve."[2]

Following that, a long debate ensued over a joint Chilean-British call for a convention on Antarctic conservation. Chile, not a signatory of the International Whaling Convention, hoped that an Antarctic agreement would take priority over the IWC in the Antarctic Treaty area. For their part, the British saw such a convention as the only way of truly protecting the wildlife of the area. The Americans were of the opinion that reaching such an agreement would take years. While acknowledging that some general rules were necessary, the Department of State did not relish the prospect of having to secure Senate ratification of a conservation agreement.[3]

The Recommendation finally adopted on conservation, I-VIII, established some temporary measures, called for further examination of the issue and in exchange for the withdrawal of the convention proposal, promised to keep the question on the agenda for the next Consultative Meeting.[4]

A year after the Canberra Meeting, the Consultative Powers met in Buenos Aires. For some reason, the intervening time does not appear to have been put to much constructive use; many of the delegations were inadequately prepared.[5]

When the Meeting addressed the conservation issue, the British again requested an international convention for preserving Antarctic wildlife.[6] The US and others (although which others are not specified) countered with the suggestion that a code would be preferable to a convention. The US still was hesitant of getting Senate ratification, and a convention would require special Presidential approval to negotiate an agreement.[7] Recommendation II-II called for more research into the Antarctic ecosystem and for a draft text of measures to be composed in preparation for the Third Consultative Meeting. Whether these "measures" would take the form of a code or a convention was left open.

Preparations for the Third Consultative Meeting began on 7 March 1963 at the First Preparatory Meeting held in Brussels (Belgium was to host the Third Consultative Meeting under Recommendation II-X). At the beginning of the discussion, the Belgian Chairman (perhaps Mr. van der Essen of the Belgian Foreign Ministry) summed up the situation by observing that although no one was against conservation, the form that such an agreement would take was a contentious issue, whether it would be a convention, a code or some other sort of concord. The British (a Mr. Carr of the FCO probably) felt that a convention would be best although Britain was prepared to accept something else.[8] British policy since Canberra appears to have remained constant; there was a firm committment to conservation in Antarctica, and although a convention was the preferred form, it was a secondary matter to providing some protection to the ecosystem. France (Mm. Justinard), Australia (Mr. Cumes) and Belgium echoed this idea to a degree, each expressing their willingness to accept either a code or a convention. Argentina (Mr. Guyer) and South Africa (Mr. Philips) opposed the idea of a convention, while Mr. Philips did stress in his rejection that South Africa was most concerned with the idea of Antarctic conservation. The discussion was suspended after Mr.

Borzov of the Soviet Union announced that the Soviets were drafting a convention for consideration.[9]

The Second Preparatory Meeting in Brussels (4 April 1963) was far from productive. The Soviets and Chileans were working on their respective draft agreements and could not say when they would be ready for circulation and discussion. For a time, Mr. van der Essen of Belgium commented on the superiority of an open convention to a code of regulations. Citing the previous season's Swiss expedition, he noted that a convention would allow wider participation than a code restricted to the Contracting Parties to the Treaty.[10] In the case of Switzerland, this was particularly important because in pursuit of absolute neutrality in international affairs, the Swiss have never joined the UN. Therefore, they must have the approval of all Consultative Powers to accede to the Treaty, hence to a code on conservation, under Article XIII paragraph 1. Difficulties of this sort would be avoided, and red tape reduced, by an open convention.

When the Third Preparatory Meeting convened on 17 June 1963, the main issue was conservation. Due to one of the many gaps in the record, one finds that the expected Soviet and Chilean draft agreements, when presented, were amendments to a British proposal hinted at in April. The exact British plan is unavailable , but the crudest guess can be made about it. The Soviet amendment replaced "Consultative Meeting" with "SCAR."[11] What SCAR was to do in place of a Consultative Meeting is not mentioned, but clearly SCAR was intended to perform a function that could have been performed by a Consultative Meeting. However, Recommendation I-IV, leaving SCAR an independent body, would clash with such an interpretation. On the other hand, SCAR may have been asked to oversee or encourage scientific research into the Antarctic ecosystem to aid in setting up regulations. This remains consistent with Recommendation I-IV in that it encourages SCAR to continue its interest in that sort of work. Perhaps this is making much out of very little, but until Antarctic documents are openly available, extrapolations of this sort are the best evaluations possible. No scrap of the Chilean amendment is available, so even less can be made of it.

It fell to Argentina's Mr. Guyer to focus on the real issue of conservation, not Britain's draft agreement (amended by others or not), but on the question of whether the final result would be a code of regulations under the Antartic Treaty or a separate, while related, convention. In response to direct questioning from Mr. Guyer, Mr. Carr for Britain and Mr. Borzov for the USSR both supported the convention approach.[12] Norway's Mr. Skarstein voiced his country's agreement with the British and Soviets. The Belgian Chairman, Mr. van der Essen, expressed his country's preference for a convention because of a difficult position constitutionally if a code were adopted as the agreement's form. Because of constitutional provisions, a code would necessitate passage of a bill by the Belgian legislature; however, as a bill, the regulations would be open to amendment. Therefore, Belgium could not guarantee adherence, word for word, to a code. A convention, though, would require only ratification, an up-or-down vote without amendment.[13]

At that point, Miss Carmichael of the US questioned whether it was the purpose of the Preparatory Meetings to come up with a specific proposal on conservation. It was the opinion of Chairman van der Essen, Mr. Carr of the UK, Mr. Cumes of Australia and Mr. Guyer of Argentina that it was, especially because Recommendation II-II called for a draft text. After a great deal of discussion of the matter, Mr. van der Essen finally proposed a separation of the question of conservation. The contents of the agreement and its form would be discussed separately.[14] This solution would allow a text to evolve, and if its form could not be agreed beforehand, it could be decided at the Consultative Meeting itself.

The Fourth Preparatory Meeting convened on 5 September 1963 to discuss the conservation issue in two distinct ways. Dealing with the contents of the agreement, Chilean and British amendments to the British draft were submitted. In addition, the Australians and Begians proposed that a comprehensive set of the various drafts and amendments be circulated in French and that a working group be established to draft a common text to reduce the numerous proposals.[15] Since a number of states' views were not available as yet, the working group would start work after the next, i.e. fifth, Preparatory Meeting, at which all views on the issue would be expressed.[16]

With the working group established to sort out the actual contents of the agreement, the matter of form arose next. Argentina's Mr. Guyer, worried about the exact distinction between a code and a convention, stated that he believed a Consultative Meeting could only make Recommendations on conservation, meaning that Meetings were not competent legally to negotiate conventions.[17] New Zealand's representative, Mr. Piddington, echoed Japan's view from the previous Preparatory Meeting[18] that the difference between a convention and a code was unimportant. Because the Treaty under Article XIII paragraph 2 allows ratification in accordance with constitutional processes, any conservation measures drawing their authority from the Treaty directly could be implemented in accordance with divergent requirements. Mr. Philips of South Africa disputed the lack of importance Mr. Piddington attached to the difference between a code and a convention. A code, argued Mr. Philips, was preferable because states opposed to a convention could accept it, and it would avoid the problems in establishing convention machinery and legal questions, e.g., "depositary government, adherence of third-party states, etc."[19]

To close off discussion, the Soviet representative, Mr. Borzov, asked for a show of hands on the question of form. Seven states favored a convention (Australia, Belgium, France, New Zealand, Norway, the UK and the USSR). The United States had no preference one way or the other, while the remaining four (Argentina, Chile, Japan and South Africa) desired a code.[20]

On 14 November 1963, the Fifth Preparatory Meeting in Brussels continued the discussion in two sections. On the substantive side of the protection of flora and fauna, the US announced that it was preparing a draft agreement. Although it was separate from the British proposal, it was to include many of the original ideas therein along with the Soviet and Chilean amendments. It was the hope of Miss Erdos of the US that this would assist the task assigned the working group of synthesizing the plethora of ideas that had been discussed.[21]

In the meantime, the British draft was still being considered. In particular, Article IV, which appears to have referred to issuing permits for the taking of specimens of protected species, was questioned. These permits would be issued, in the French version, by the *"authorité compétent."* Although the British defined this as the government whose nationals were going to take the specimens, this terminology was later to become a sticking point.[22] The issuing of permits for a purpose like this is part of sovereignty, the regulation of activities within a state's territory.

On the question of what form the agreement would take, the most important development was an American decision to press for "agreed measure" not a convention in the strict sense. The rationale underlying this was the fear that a series of separate treaties would develop and that the Antarctic Treaty itself would be diminished. Washington envisioned these "agreed measures" being incorporated into a Recommendation. In addition to securing governmental approval under Article IX paragraph 4, the measures would remain open to accession by other powers if they accede to the Treaty. Once again, Chairman van der Essen raised Belgium's constitutional difficulties in the matter and expressed his opinion that the American proposal would not resolve the matter of form.[23]

The Sixth Preparatory Meeting of 24 January 1964 began with the working group for the protection of Antarctic flora and fauna. Mr. van der Essen urged that the purpose of the group would be to unify all of the proposals in circulation, including the US draft of 12 December 1963.[24] Argentina and Australia reminded all delegations that flexibility was necessary for the synthesis to success. Additionally, Australia and Britain stated that they would consider the results of the working group as a basis for discussion and not a binding agreement. Decision on form, for them, would be reserved as a prerogative for the Consultative Meeting to decide.[25]

With regard to the form side of the conservation matter, Argentina rejected the US proposal for "agreed measures" and demanded a convention. Australia responded by saying that "agreed measures" could be defined broadly to mean either a code or a convention. Belgium had more to say about its constitutional problem; especially, its constitution required any penal deterrent to be the result of legislative action. A convention would be law by decree. A solution was offered by Mr. van der Essen, a dual procedure. A "mini-treaty" (*"courte convention"* in the original) whereby all signatories agreed to pass laws to implement the agreed measures. It would remain open to accession by all Contracting Parties to the Treaty. In this way, states requiring parliamentary acts to implement the provisions could meet these obligations while those without such difficulties could directly enforce the measures. Pro-code South Aftica stated that it could support such an approach, but the US expressed its concern that, in the end, identical rules would not be in force for each state.[26]

Almost exactly a year after the First Preparatory Meeting, the seventh in the series was held, 5 March 1964. The Preparatory Meeting began with a brief report on the efforts of the working group in synthesizing the various draft proposals. The records of the work of this group are unavailable, but for the purposes of the matter at hand, the evolution of the System, they are only marginally relevant. How the conservation agreements are tied to the Treaty is far more important than what specific provisions were initially suggested. In any case, the final result of these negotiations will be discussed in detail further on in the chapter.

On the matter of form, the American draft of Agreed Measures (later adopted with some alterations as Recommendation III-VIII) achieved a major change in the thinking of many states. Britain more or less abandoned its own draft in favor of the Agreed Measures as a basis of discussion; the French delegate, Mm. Justinard, agreed whole-heartedly with the American aproach and said that a separate convention was not necessary. Even Belgium was prepared to accept the Agreed Measures over a convention. Mr. van der Essen was at pains to point out that as Agreed Measures, they would only bind the Belgian government and not its citizens, there would be no difficulties because all Belgian expeditions were government-sponsored. Sponsorship could be made contingent on acceptance of the Treaty and the Agreed Measures as a Recommendation. Thus, the constitutional difficulties could be overcome. New Zealand, South Africa, Norway, Japan, Australia, the Soviet Union were all prepared to use the Agreed Measures as a basis for discussion.[27] This revolution in favor of something less than a convention was not so much the result of US pressure but rather a realization that a convention could not be unanimously agreed. The US draft, having been drawn from all the previous proposals, was accepted on whatever merits it had and not at the insistence of its sponsor.

Under the heading of new business, Britain proposed that SCAR be invited to issue tri-annual reports on the conditions of Antarctic flora and fauna in support of the Agreed Measures. Although there was no discussion or elaboration,[28] this underlines the committment the British had to conservation in the Antarctic. SCAR reports on the state of the indigenous species would further aid the Consultative Parties in their efforts at conservation.

The Eighth Preparatory Meeting on 3 April 1964 saw the protection of flora and fauna to be more or less settled. The working group was progressing in unifying the proposals. As for form, the last state to make a decision, Chile, said it preferred a convention (a reversal in its thinking since the Fourth Preparatory Meeting), but it could accept the Agreed Measures format if that were what was necessary to provide agreement.[29] Whatever reasons existed for the about-face on Chile's part, Chilean flexibility ensured the success of the Preparatory Meetings' handling of the problem and showed a genuine concern for the Antarctic biosphere. As this brought unanimity on the question of form, the issue was settled as far as the Preparatory Meetings were concerned.

This is not to say that the matter of conservation was over for the Preparatory Meetings. Britain's proposal for tri-annual SCAR reports remained, and to this the British desired to add discussions on the protection of pelagic seals to those on flora and fauna. However, these were deferred until the next Preparatory Meeting.[30] At that gathering, 28 April 1964, those British proposals were added to the agenda under the heading of protection of fauna and flora.[31]

In part, this explains why the Agreed Measures from the Third Consultative Meeting had to be followed by an agreement on pelagic seals in 1972. The discussion had progressed in two stages, and pelagic seals were not taken into consideration until after the Agreed Measures were well underway. On the one hand, this shows a foresightedness on the part of the British in bringing the matter up for discussion, but one wonders why these species were not included from the very beginning.

Clearly the longest debate of the Third Consultative Meeting in June 1964 was that on the Agreed Measures. In general, Argentina and Chile, to a lesser degree, would allow nothing in the Agreed Measures to hint at a lessening of national sovereignty. Australia tried very hard to extend the provisions of the agreement to extend to the high seas, but their efforts were defeated by the opposition of the superpowers and of the South Americans. The implementary clauses put Britain and Australia at the head of a group opposed to giving the US further responsibilities (it was already the depositary government for the Treaty). "This reflected their habitual view that Washington should not be allowed to 'take over the Treaty'."[32]

Beginning with the preamble, the working paper was entitled *Agreed Measures for the Conservation of Living Resources in Antarctica*. Britain, for precision's sake, wanted the "living resources" to read "wildlife" in the English language version. The US resisted this, and a compromise led to the title being *Agreed Measures for the Conservation of Antarctic Fauna and Flora*. The preamble, though, is almost exactly what the Soviet Union proposed on 4 June 1963.[33]

Article I of the Agreed Measures defines the area of application as that South of 60° South Latitude, but keeping the freedom of the high seas. This is the same as that of the Antarctic Treaty. On 4 June 1963, the Soviets proposed amending this to include wording declaring Antarctica an "International Wild Life Reserve." Chile accepted the Soviet idea, to a degree, in that the area should be a "nature sanctuary," rejecting the connotation and denotation of "international." While the US and Britain could accept this, Argentine resistance kept it out of the final draft.[34]

Article II defines: 1) native animal, 2) native bird, 3) native plant, 4) appropriate authority, and 5) contracting government. Argentina was concerned about the concept of an appropriate authority but did not force a change.[35]

The shortest article is the third, but it carries a great deal of importance. While reading simply, "Each Participating Government shall take appropriate action to carry out these Agreed Measures," it addressed the whole issue of form. Essentially, it fudges the point, allowing Belgium and others with constitutional difficulties with certain forms to approach the agreement in any way they needed to put the Agreed Measures into effect.

Articles IV and V are simply measures of practicality. Article IV seeks to ensure that personnel in Antarctica are aware of the provision in the Agreed Measures. Article V is a common sense principle that in the event of life-threatening circumstances, the Agreed Measures are not applicable.[36]

By Article VI, the first truly contentious article, native wildlife is made sacrosanct and may only be interfered with under a permit. Australia and the US endeavored to get even more protection for female animals by further restricting permits issued for them. An excellent concept due to the different reproductive capabilities of males and females, this proposal failed because of the difficulty that exists in distinguishing gender in Antarctic animals.[37]

Article VII is a thoroughly non-controversial piece striving to preserve the normal living conditions of Antarctic animals. The stronger American draft, slightly revised, was adopted over the British version.[38] Both of these, though, drew heavily on the Soviet regulations from 1962.[39]

Article VIII establishes Specially Protected Areas (SPA). This simply restricts permits further than normal. It generated no controversy in Brussels.

Since man is not the only alien life form on Antarctic expeditions, but he is accompanied by sled dogs, bacteria and other parasites, Article IX was drafted. The intent is to prevent these alien species from upsetting the natural balance in Antarctica. Such a sensible proposal, not surprisingly, brought no debate.

Article X of the Agreed Measures recalls Article X of the Treaty almost verbatim. Since the wording was agreed to in the Treaty, it was quietly accepted in the Agreed Measures as well. The intent of each is to make sure nonparty states obey the regulations and provisions of each agreement. Article XI expands this to ships in the Southern Ocean.

Article XII provides for an exchange of information on regulations in force, data on specimens taken and data on the status of various species. The chief difficulty here was to keep this exchange similar to other exchanges of data to ensure its approval.[40] The US proposal for meetings on the issue was, therefore, defeated.[41]

The formal provisions of the Agreed Measures are contained in Article XIII. Of most importance is paragraph 2 concerning the accession of states to the Agreed Measures. The US and others felt that any state eligible to accede to the Treaty should be allowed to endorse the Agreed Measures separately. Australia asserted that accession should only be open to Contracting Parties to the Treaty. The Soviets, adopting their traditional view, believed, that all states should be allowed to accede. Problems existed with all of these. If independent accession were allowed, a legal question arises, viz., what legal right does a non-Treaty state have to an interest in Antarctica causing it to accede? If non-Treaty states can accede to specific Recommendations? What will happen if Recommendations exist for Consultative or Contracting Parties only?[42] In the end, the Australian view prevailed.[43]

The amendment process, Article XIV, requires unanimous consent. However, the US proposed a certain flexibility so that the technical annexes, concerning quotas on each species, etc., could be easily amended. Thus diplomatic channels can be used in addition to Recommendations of Consultative Meetings for the purpose of amending the Agreed Measures. A long time was required to explain this, but once the point was clear, the US proposal "won not only support, but even enthusiasm."[44]

Despite a quite respectable amount of environmental protection that would result from the Agreed Measures, they were not enough because they would take time to implement.[45] To make sure that something would cover the intervening time, the British advanced a proposal whereby the governments would immediately implement them and approve them later. This seems to have been a case of overzealousness on the British part for Antarctic conservation. The US, quite rightly, convinced Britain and the others that the doubtful legality of this would not accomplish the purpose. Instead, the Americans suggested that, until approved, the Agreed Measures would serve as voluntary regulations.[46] Recommendation III-IX embodies this concept.

In order to implement the Agreed Measures successfully, a great deal more had to be known about the Antarctic ecosystem. To this end, SCAR was encouraged in Recommendation III-X to promote research on this point, and as per Britain's proposal, issue reports on this matter.[47]

Scarcely had one conservation point been settled than another one began. Pelagic sealing, i.e., the taking of seals at sea, was one of the most debated items at the Third Consultative Meeting involving both freedom of the high seas and commercial activities. The story here proves, if nothing else, that the curse of Babel still exists.

Australia had insisted that the Agreed Measures would mean nothing if animals on the Antarctic pack ice were not protected; the overwhelming majority of the seal population falls into this category. Norway, supported by the Soviets, took a predictable stand in saying that it would go sealing in the Antarctic and had every right to do so. The US and UK tried to mediate and eventually reached enough common ground for a working group on the matter to be worthwhile. The Australian, Norwegian, British, American and Soviet Representatives succeeded in coming up with a draft working paper that would have provided for voluntary controls on pelagic sealing.

When this draft was submitted to all the delegations, the Chileans rejected the proposal out of hand. Another working group met, then, composed of the original working group's members plus the Chileans. No progress was made on a new paper. Eventually, the Soviets had to force the issue due to time constraints in asking for instructions from Moscow; either the Recommendation was approved as it was, or the Soviets would defer the matter of pelagic sealing until the next Meeting. Chile insisted that it would agree to an item on pelagic sealing, it was in favor of the principle of restricting pelagic sealing, but the present draft

could not be accepted by Chile. At that point, a member of the US delegation noticed what was termed a "gross error in the translation"[48] of the
Spanish version. In the Spanish text, the Recommendation was to affect
the whole area South of 60° South. This differed from the other versions
which stated that only the pack ice in that area were to be affected. When
this discrepancy was corrected, the text "passed in the plenary without
debate."[49]   Recommendation III-XI calls for voluntary regulations on
pelagic sealing and for consideration of the issue at the next Consultative
Meeting in Santiago.

At the Santiago Preparatory Meeting, 5-9 September 1966, conservation remained on the agenda in a number of ways. There were various
proposals on fine tuning the Agreed Measures, and there was the entire
question of pelagic sealing. At the Preparatory Meeting, the purpose was
not so much to settle points so that the Consultative Meeting could give
its rubber stamp approval as it was to agree on what the agenda would be.
Consequently, the preparations for Santiago decided less than those for
Brussels.

Ever the leaders on conservation issues, the British had circulated
some ideas on pelagic sealing well before the September gathering, and
they had discussions with all the other delegations privately. Then, they
drafted a paper that concerned itself only with the substantive question of
sealing, having learned that form could delay things from the Agreed
Measures negotiations.   Their proposal tried to protect the seals by
establishing a maximum sustainable yield (i.e., the largest number of seals
that could be taken before reproduction could not replace the harvest),
limiting the hunting of seals on pack ice, defining quotas and hunting
zones and creating closed seasons on sealing.   Norway, involved in
sealing at both poles, favored the British proposals and would review the
specifics of it for the Fourth Consultative Meeting.   Chiefly, Norway
wanted more research into the pelagic seals of Antarctica to make the
quotas, maximum sustainable yields, etc., as accurate as possible. New
Zealand adopted a similar line in questioning the validity of the British
figures although supporting the proposal in general.[50]

Although the British endeavored to keep the matter of form out of the
debate by their proposal, it arose when the Australians, despite their
approval of the British ideas, expressed their belief that Article VI of the
Treaty, concerning freedom of the high seas, precluded an agreement
within the framework set out in the Treaty. South Africa differed with
Australia on this point saying that something along the lines of the
Agreed Measures would be the best approach. The US, having assisted in
the drafting of the British proposal, supported the suggestions it
contained.   Like Norway, the US wanted more research into the matter
being particularly concerned that by regulating sealing the Consultative
Powers might do damage to the ecosystem as a whole. The US, in addressing the matter of form, suggested that the Santiago Consultative Meeting
evolve a text of a convention but that the agreement should be signed
separately from the Treaty's mechanisms. In voicing their support of the
proposals, the Japanese believed that Article VI would require a separate

convention. For their part, the French supported the draft as agreed measures, as did Argentina, Belgium and Chile. The USSR felt that discussions were necessary but had no position on the form it should finally take. With so much support, the item was placed on the agenda without objection.[51]

It is important to note here that even those states most concerned with protecting the Antarctic environment, Britain for one, did not object to the idea of taking pelagic seals. Their only concern was that this should be done in a way that did not damage the ecosystem as a whole. Had they taken a more dogmatic stand, sealing states, Norway primarily, would undoubtedly have blocked the entire proposal. Indeed, the British approach was of benefit to the sealing states in that it would prevent over-harvesting of the seals and thereby it would insure that the sealing industry would not ruin itself.

Further on in the Preparatory Meeting, the Consultative Powers addressed the Agreed Measures, Recommendation III-VIII. Chile introduced the question but did not elaborate on its intentions at the time. Britain took this to mean that reports on how the Agreed Measures had been implemented were to be prepared for the Consultative Meeting, something both the UK and the US would favor. It was put on the agenda without objection. In private, though, the Chileans stated their intention to amend Article II paragraph (d) of the Agreed Measures, that part that defines "appropriate authority." Britain said that this could not be done because Parliament was in the process of ratifying the Agreed Measures, and any amendment would damage Her Majesty's Government's efforts to steer the Recommendation through. The US told Chile it did not sympathize with the desire to amend Article II. As a result, "[a] very slight modification of the Chilean position was noted."[52] The usual South American solidarity on matters touching on sovereignty was only half-hearted this time because Argentina had already ratified the Agreed Measures. In addition to this point on the Agreed Measures, the Consultative Powers decided to discuss the technical annexes to the Recommendation.[53]

When the Fourth Consultative Meeting began on 3 November 1966, the Consultative Powers had the same conservation points to discuss as they had at the Preparatory Meeting: the technical annexes to the Agreed Measures, the proposed amendment of the Agreed Measures and pelagic sealing.

Coming first among conservation issues, the technical annexes to the Agreed Measures generated little controversy. They centered themselves on the establishment of Specially Protected Areas (SPA) and Specially Protected Species (SPS). SCAR had recently completed a report on these, and the unanimous agreement of the scientists on a scientific question carried considerable influence among the diplomats. Recommendations IV-1 to IV-17 inclusive cover the establishment of these SPAs and SPSs.[54]

The amendment of the Agreed Measures more than made up for the total agreement on the technical annexes. As at the Preparatory Meeting, Chile objected to the term "appropriate authority" in Article II and desired to amend it; Britain, still in the process of ratifying the Agreed Measures would allow no change in the text. It was pointed out at the Preparatory Meeting that the Spanish text read "competent" and not "appropriate" authority. The US offered a change in the translation, but Chile argued that that did not solve the problem.[55] Chile continued to insist that the words be removed. A few attempts were made to bridge the gap. The French offered a draft Recommendation to define "appropriate", but Chile rejected it. The Americans and Australians used their good offices but to no avail. Chile offered a Recommendation on how permits should be issued, but as that was tantamount to an amendment, the British could not accept it. When no settlement seemed possible, Chile and Britain agreed to disagree. Chile would withdraw its amendments, and after Parliament had ratified the Agreed Measures, Britain promised to seek an agreement with Chile.[56]

On the question of the permits themselves, New Zealand had two proposals, one on coordinating the issuing of permits and another establishing a common form of reporting data on specimens taken under permit. On the latter point, agreement came as the result of a working group's (Argentina, Australia, Britain, New Zealand and the United States) alterations of SCAR's suggestions. The former received unanimous support in principle and wording of a Recommendation rather than its substance was the focus of debate.[57]

The issue of controlling pelagic sealing was more contentious. The UK and Norway both wanted to institute regulations in some form that were based on the best possible data.[58] The US, favoring the same and interim guidelines with the gathering of more scientific data, sponsored a moratorium on pack ice sealing.[59] This received extremely heavy support from Chile and embodied the view of the majority. Britain had made it clear before the Meeting, though, that it could not accept a moratorium. So, Chile proposed adopting Recommendations from SCAR's IX Meeting. The US and UK preferred voluntary restraints,[60] a view that was more or less embodied in Recommendation IV-21.

On the eternal question of form, Argentina, Japan and South Africa supported a separate convention due to Artice VI of the Treaty. The US agreed but felt form could be decided later. Argentina demanded that a Recommendation specifying a separate convention be approved, but the US convinced them to accept more general language.[61]

There were a few other points concerning pelagic sealing. The working group that drafted Recommendation IV-21 removed a paragraph of Belgian origin calling on governments to take appropriate action in controlling pelagic sealing. No reference was made to the high seas because of Treaty Article VI. Finally, the US desired more protection for seals near SPAs, but this brought up the issue of territorial seas, therefore, of sovereignty, and the matter had to be dropped.[62]

In preparation for the Fifth Consultative Meeting in Paris, the first Preparatory Meeting was held in mid-December 1967. The issue of pelagic sealing was placed on the agenda for the Consultative Meeting as a matter of course because it was mandated by Recommendations adopted in

Santiago, as were the Agreed Measures.[63]

Conservation was not brought up again until the Fourth Preparatory Meeting on 26 July 1968. Then on the issue of the Agreed Measures, Chile proposed to "eliminate every work concerning the problem of sovereignty,"[64] i.e., "appropriate authority" in Article II of the Agreed Measures. Britain expressed its willingness to clear the matter up, having ratified the agreement, but the British noted that few other states had done so.[65]

At the Fifth Preparatory Meeting, 24 September 1968, the Chilean desire to amend the Agreed Measures again came up. This time, the Soviets requested that the Chileans withdraw the item on making amendments from the agenda. Chile refused.[65]

After the formalities of the opening of the Fifth Consultative Meeting in Paris on 18 November 1968, reports on the implementation of the Agreed Measures were given. Constitutionally, the USSR, France, Norway and South Africa had only to approve Recommendation III-VIII for the Agreed Measures to enter into force for them, and they had done this. For the others, domestic legislation of one kind or another was required, and it was being considered. Australia and New Zealand, however, had halted their legislative processes pending Chile's drive to amend Article II.[66]

Next, the delegates tried to resolve the question of pelagic sealing. The UK, supported by the US, circulated the SCAR general meeting's proposals.[67] Because of Norway's intention to send a sealing expedition, the Consultative Powers were under considerable pressure to come up with regulations. The Soviets, throughout, were rigid, demanding adoption of the SCAR version verbatim. Eventually, they relented and allowed Norway's cosmetic changes.[68] Despite this, drafting an entire agreement in such a short time just proved impossible. The Soviets could not agree with the UK on the accession clause; the Soviets wanted any state to be able to accede while the UK wanted only UN members to be eligible. Also, there were disputes on entry into force and on amend- ment procedures. Completion of the draft was deferred to the next Consultative Meeting.[69] The question of form was not at issue because the agreement would, of necessity, limit freedom of the high seas; so, a separate treaty was a necessity. At least part of the Soviet intractability was a part of a personal dispute between Simsarian of the US and Treshnikov of the USSR. Additionally, it is customary for the ambassadors to the host country to head delegations but only in name. Mr. Treshnikov had further problems in that Soviet Ambassador Zorine took his responsibility more seriously than was the custom, thereby forcing Treshnikov to be more rigid.[70]

On amending the Agreed Measured, Chile received only partial satisfaction. The US was prepared to accept any change that did not imply recognition of a territorial claim or limit the US right to exclusive control over permits for American scientists.[71] However, the Soviets maintained, and were supported by many others including the US, that Chile was trying to assert a territorial claim.[72] Recommendation V-6 amended Article II paragraph (d) by adding:

> *The function of an authorized person will be carried out within the framework of the Antarctic Treaty. They will be carried out exclusively in accordance with scientific principles and will have as their sole purpose the effective protection of Antarctic fauna and flora in accordance with these Agreed Measures.*[73]

Paragraph (e) was also changed so that "appropriate authority" was referred to as defined above.[74] This was an amendment but it fell far short of what Chile had asked for in Santiago.

At this point, the American sources dry up, and the inside workings on the pelagic sealing negotiations must be concluded based on the few facts available and reasonable surmise. Enough exists to finish the history, if somewhat unsatisfyingly.

According to Article X of the Convention on the Conservation of Antarctic Seals, the agreement was the result of a conference in London in February of 1972. That places it between the Sixth Consultative Meeting in Tokyo in 1970 and the Seventh Consultative Meeting in Wellington from 30 October to 10 November 1972. Yet the Tokyo Recommendations do not mention pelagic sealing. The only conservation Recommendation was VI-4 which covered the impact of humans on Antarctica and requesting SCAR to study the matter.[75] From this, it is reasonable to deduce that the negotiations for the seal agreement were conducted separately from the Consultative Meetings after Paris. Despite that, the sealing agreement ties itself closely to the Treaty; under the terms on the 1972 convention, SCAR is invited to carry out several functions involving the gathering and exchange of data, much as under Recommendations of the Consultative Meetings. In addition, and most telling, the participants at the London Conference were exclusively Consultative Powers under the Antarctic Treaty.[76]

As a final note to the sealing issue, most of the Consultative Powers had no intention ever to harvest seals in Antarctica. Despite that, they felt a need to regulate it in preservation of the ecosystem, at least in principle. In practice, the seventh ratification reached the British (the depositary government) six years after the text was approved, and the seventh was the one necessary to put the agreement into force.[77] So although there was a safeguard in existence, it did not have legal force behind it until 1978.

NOTES

[1]United States, National Science Foundation, "Trip Report to the First Antarctic Treaty Consultative Meeting", National Archives of the United States, Center for Polar Records, RG307, Box 29, File 102.1.2, p. 1.

[2]United States, Department of State, "Draft Position Paper on Conservation of Antarctic Living Resources", RG 307, Box 29, File 102.1.1.

[3]National Science Foundation, "Trip Report ... First Consultative Meeting ...", p. 3.

[4]*Ibid.* Recommendations are identified by two numbers. The first Roman numeral designates the Consultative Meeting out of which it arose; the second, either Roman or Arabic, numeral designates its position among all the Recommendations from that particular Meeting.

[5]United States, National Science Foundation, "Trip Report to the Second Consultative Meeting", RG 307, Box 28, File 102.1, p. 1.

[6]United States, United States Navy, "Memorandum for the Record on the Second Consultative Meeting", Office of the Chief of Naval Operations, 6 August 1962, National Archives of the United States, Records of the Naval Operating Forces, US Naval Support Force, Antarctica, History and Research Division, Research Files, Reprints and Publications, Record Group 313, Box 79, File 2A112, p. 2. Hereafter such records will be cited solely by Record Group 313, with box and file numbers.

[7]National Science Foundation, "Trip Report to the Second Consultative Meeting", p. 1.

[8]United States, Department of State, Division of Language Services, "Minutes of the First Preparatory Meeting for the Third Antarctic Treaty Consultative Meeting", LS no. 53895 RXV-RXVIII in French. RG 307, Box 29, File 102D. The record of the Brussels negotiations are the only ones complete enough to offer much in the way of names of the participating diplomats.

[9]*Ibid.*

[10]United States, Department of State, "Minutes of the Second Meeting in Preparation for the Third Antarctic Treaty Consultative Meeting", Enclosure to Airgram A-1262, US Embassy Brussels to Department of State Washington, 26 August 1963, RG 307, Box 18, File 102D.

[11]United States, Department of State, "Procès-Verbal de la Troisème Réunion Préparatoire a la IIIe Réunion Consultative De L'Antarctique", Enclosure to Airgram A-17, US Embassy Brussels to Department of State Washington, 5 July 1963, RG 307, Box 18, File 102D, p. 2.

[12]*Ibid.*, p. 3.

[13]*Ibid.*

[14]*Ibid.*, pp. 3-4.

[15]United States, Department of State, Division of Language Services, "Minutes of the Fourth Meeting in Preparation for the Third Antarctic Consultative Meeting", LS no. 8421, T-39, R-XVIII in French, RG 307, Box 18, File 102D, p. 6.

[16]*Ibid.*, p. 3.

[17]*Ibid.*, pp. 6-7.

[18]Department of State, "Procès-Verbal de la Troisième Réunion Préparatoire ...", p. 4.

62

[19]Department of State, Division of Language Services, "Minutes of the Fourth Meeting in Prepartion ...", p. 8. In the opinion of the author Piddington's reading of the Treaty's ratification clause was perfectly correct from a legal standpoint, but Philips' concern was political, not legal.

[20]*Ibid.*, pp. 8-9.

[21]United States, Department of State, "Procès-Verbal de la 5ème Réunion Préparatoire a la IIIe Réunion de L'Antarctique", Enclosure to Airgram A-606, US Embassy Brussels to Department of State Washington, 23 December 1963, RG 307, Box 18, File 102D, pp. 1-2.

[22]*Ibid.*, p. 2.

[23]*Ibid.*, pp. 4-6.

[24]United States, Department of State, "Procès-Verbal de la 6ème Réunion Préparatoire a la IIIe Réunion Consultative", Enclosure to Air- gram A-743, US Embassy Brussels to Department of State Washington, January 1964, RG 307, Box 18, File 102D, p. 2.

[25]*Ibid.*, pp. 2-3.

[26]*Ibid.*, pp. 3-5.

[27]United States, Department of State, "Procès-Verbal de la 7ème Réunion Préparatoire a la IIIe Réunion Consultative", Enclosure to Airgram A-981, US Embassy Brussels to Department of State Washington, 6 March 1964, RG 307, Box 18, File 102D, pp. 1-3.

[28]*Ibid.*, p. 8.

[29]United States, Department of State, "Procès-Verbal de la 8ème Réunion Préparatoire a la IIIe Réunion Consultative", Enclosure to Airgram A-1070, US Embassy Brussels to Department of State Washington, 30 April 1964, RG 307, Box 18, File 102D, p. 1.

[30]*Ibid.*, pp. 6-8.

[31]United States, Department of State, "Procès-Verbal de la 9ème Réunion Préparatoire a la IIIe Réunion Consultative", Enclosure to Airgram A-1090, US Embassy Brussels to Department of State Washington, May 1964, RG 307, Box 18, File 102D, pp. 2-3.

[32]United States, Department Department of State, "Report of the US Delegation to the Third Consultative Meeting under the Antarctic Treaty", RG 307, Box 18, File 102D.

[33]United Kingdom, Foreign and Commonwealth Office, "Proposed Agreement on the Conservation of Wildlife in the Antarctic", 28 February 1964, RG 307, Box 29, File 102D.

[34]Department of State, "Report of the US Delegation to the Third Consultative Meeting", pp. 5-7.

[35]*Ibid.*, p. 6.

[36]No debate seems to have been generated by Articles III-V.

[37]United States, Department of State, "Position Papers of the United States for the Third Consultative Meeting," RG 313, Box 79, File 2A112.

[38]Foreign and Commonwealth Office, "Proposed Agreement ...", pp. 9-10.

[39]United States, Department of State, Division of Language Services, "Notes on the Draft Convention for the Conservation of Live Resources of Antarctica", LS no. 58402, T-21/R-13, Russian, RG 307, Box 18, File 102D. For the Soviet regulations see, United States, Department of State, "Soviet Draft Regulations on Flora and Fauna", July 1962, RG 313, Box 29, File 102.1.

[40]Department of State, "Report of the US Delegation to the Third Consultative Meeting ...", p. 7.

[41]Foreign and Commonwealth Office, "Proposed Agreement ...", p. 14.

[42]Department of State, "Report of the US Delegation to the Third Consultative Meeting ...", p. 7.

[43]Article XII, paragraph 2 of the Agreed Measures.

[44]Department of State, "Report of the US Delegation to the Third Consultative Meeting ...", p. 7.

[45]For example, as late as 1975, the US had yet to approve them. See Antarctic Treaty, "Final Report of the Eighth Antarctic Consultative Meeting", National Archives of the United States, Center for Polar Archives, Reference File.

[46]Department of State, "Report of the US Delegation to the Third Consultative Meeting ...", p. 8.

[47]Ibid.

[48]Ibid., p. 9.

[49]Ibid.

[50]United States, Department of State, "Preparatory Delegation Report" [Fourth Consultative Meeting preparations], RG 307, Box 18, File 102D, p.4.

[51]Ibid., pp. 4-6.

[52]Ibid., p. 8.

[53]Ibid.

[54]United States, Department of State, "Report of the US Delegation to the Fourth Consultative Meeting: Annexes to the Agreed Measure for the Conservation of Antarctic

64

Fauna and Flora", RG 307, Box 19, File 102D.

[55]United States, Department of State, "Position Paper for the Fourth Consultative Meeting: Chilean Amendments to the Agreed Measures", RG 313, Box 80, File 2A112.

[56]United States, Department of State, "Report of the US Delegation to the Fourth Consultative Meeting: Agreed Measures for the Conservation of Antarctic Fauna and Flora," RG 307, Box 19, File 102D.

[57]United States, Department of State, "Position Paper for the Fourth Consultative Meeting: Implementation of Article XIII, (1) (d) of the Agreed Measures", RG 313 Box 80, File 2A112; "Report of the US Delegation to the Fourth Consultative Meeting: Coordination of Permits", RG 307, Box 19, File 102D; "Position Paper for the Fourth Consultative Meeting: Coordination of Permits", RG 313, Box 80, File 2A112; and "Report of the US Delegation to the Fourth Consultative Meeting: Implementation of Article XIII (1) (d) of the Agreed Measures", RG 307, Box 19, File 102D.

[58]United States, Department of State, "Report of the US Delegation to the Fourth Consultative Meeting: Pelagic Sealing", RG 307, Box 19, File 102D.

[59]United States, Department of State, "Position Paper for the Fourth Consultative Meeting: Pelagic Sealing", RG 313, Box 80, File 2A112.

[60]Ibid.

[61]Department of State, "Report ... Pelagic Sealing".

[62]Ibid.

[63]United States, Department of State, "Minutes of the First Preparatory Meeting for the Fifth Consultative Meeting", Enclosure to Airgram A-1076, US Embassy London to Department of State Washington, 26 December 1967, RG 307, Box 20, File 102D.

[64]United States, Department of State, "Minutes of the Fourth Preparatory Meeting for the Fifth Consultative Meeting", Enclosure to Airgram-2426, US Embassy Paris to Department of State Washington, 26 July 1968, RG 307, Box 20, File 102D.

[65]United States, Department of State, "Notes on the Fifth Preparatory Meeting [for the Fifth Consultative Meeting]", Letter to James Simsarian from John H. Buehler, Assistant Scientific Attaché, US Embassy Paris, 22 September 1968, RG 307, Box 20, File 102D.

[66]United States, Department of State, "Report of the US Delegation to the Fifth Consultative Meeting under Article IX of the Antarctic Treaty", RG 307, Box 20, File 102D, p. 3.

[67]For early drafts, see SCAR, Polar Record. (Vol. 14, no. 92, May 1969), pp. 670-5.

[68]Department of State, "Report...Fifth Consultative Meeting ...", pp. 6-9.

[69]Recommendation V-6.

[70]United States, National Science Foundation, "Memorandum from Henry S. Francis to Charles Maechling", 19 February 1969, RG 307, Box 20, File 102D.

[71]United States, Department of State, "Position Paper on Amending the Agreed Measures", RG 307, Box 20, File 102D.

[72]Department of State, "Report ... Fifth Consultative Meeting ...", p. 10.

[73]Recommendation V-6.

[74]*Ibid.*

[75]Report on the Sixth Consultative Meeting, Tokyo, 1970, *Polar Record.* (Vol. 15, no. 98), pp. 729-42.

[76]F.M. Auburn, *Antarctic Law and Politics*, p. 210.

[77]*Ibid.*, p. 211.

CHAPTER VI
THE ROLE OF MEETINGS OF EXPERTS

From the beginning of Antarctic exploartion, scientific research has been a part, indeed the main part, of human activity in the region. As demonstrated by the IGY, national research efforts are enhanced greatly when nations cooperate in research. This is acknowledged in Article IX paragraph 2 sections B and C, which call for the "facilitation of scientific research in Antarctica" and "the facilitation of international scientific cooperation in Antarctica." For the Treaty System, this facilitation has been one of its most important and successful efforts. That is not to say that this has been an easy task. In particular, it affected the relationship between the scientists and the diplomats.

Because pure scientific research is highly specialized, it is not surprising that some of the Antarctic System's business has been of a fairly technical nature. The diplomats are not competent to judge some of the scientific issues that arise, and they would be the first to admit it. Quite resonably therefore, technical matters are left to the experts in the particular fields. Yet this results in a structural problem for the System. Do these Meetings of Experts count as Consultative Meetings? Do the Recommendations of the scientists carry the same weight as those of the diplomats? Can the scientists conduct their own diplomacy in technical matters? The first years of the Treaty had to find an answer to these questions. The problem was to allow the interests of the scientific community to be upheld while at the same time safe-guarding the other aspects of the Treaty.

The first hint of the problem's existence arose in Canberra under an agenda item on logistics. Australia seems to have raised the issue by pressing for broader cooperation in logistical matters. Exactly what this meant is unclear, but the US feared becoming involved in a situation whereby the US Navy would be forced to give logistical support to all other nations in the Antarctic. Since the Soviets were about to ask for over-flight rights in New Zealand and Australian air space and for a staging base in New Zealand, they supported bilateral and multi-lateral assistance measures for logistics. If successful, this would have allowed them to use Christchurch, New Zealand and America's McMurdo base as support posts for Mirny station.[1] In the end, Recommendation I-VII did not go that far; it merely called for exchange of various data of logistical significance and for consideration of a meeting of logistical experts.

Later in the Canberra Meeting, the Australian delegation came forward to propose a Recommendation calling for a meeting of telecommunications experts. Of chief concern were meteorological reports because the time lag between the actual taking of the measurements and the receipt of the report often made data too old to be of value to forecasters. Since the

US had already offered to hold such a meeting in Washington, it was not a question of whether to meet but rather of establishing a frame of reference for the meeting.[2] Recommendation I-XI, resulting from some dissatisfaction with SCAR's handling of the issue,[3] established that a Meeting of Experts should consider many technical points but that agenda matters and invitations be decided on by the governments of the Consultative Powers later.[4]

At the Buenos Aires Meeting, the Meetings of Experts issue advanced very little. This was chiefly due to the fact that the Consultative Powers did not realize that a problem existed. Moreover, no Experts' Meeting had been held since Canberra, and so there had been no opportunity for the problem to make itself seen.

In any case, the Australians remained as desirous of a Meeting of Experts to address radio communications as they had been the year before. In Buenos Aires, they submitted a draft agenda for the Meeting of Experts.[5] Since arrangements were under way, Recommendation II-III only set the date for the Washington Meeting of Experts for between May and 31 August 1963.

On logistical matters, the Meeting's discussion occurred with the knowledge that SCAR was staging a symposium on the exchange of information on logistics in Boulder, Colorado during August 1962. Both Argentina and Australia wanted a similar meeting to be held in the latter half of 1963, but under the aegis of the Consultative Powers instead of SCAR.[6] The Americans were hesitant about the proposal fearing that the final result of that sort of gathering would be an obligation to support other countries' programs at the expense of America's own.[7] The contents of Recommendation II-V provided for consultations on holding a governmentally sponsored Meeting of Experts on logistics. The Soviets pointed out to the Americans that no such Meeting would occur because of the likelihood of SCAR's symposium exhausting the subject.[8] This may in part explain American acquiescence to the Recommendation. However, the American fears of being saddled with all the logistical responsibilities seems unjustified. After all, the Treaty requires unanimity for the approval of Recommendations. The US could simply have refused anything requiring their unwilling support.

In the preparations for the Brussels Consultative Meeting, the issue of the role of Experts' Meeting became an identifiable problem. However, the problem was not sighted until the first Preparatory Meetings had concluded.

At the First Preparatory Meeting on 7 March 1963, the matter of telecommunications did not arise because invitations to the Washington Conference had been sent out. After this was reported by the Americans, logistics was taken up. As expressed by Chairman van der Essen of Belgium, the issue was divided along two lines of thought. The first noted that logistics was a governmental responsibility and therefore a governmental meeting would be in order. The second held that the SCAR symposium in August 1962 had made a further meeting extraneous; as the Soviets had predicted, this second line of reasoning claimed that SCAR's symposium had exhausted all the material. After van der Essen's comments, Argentina's Mr. Guyer stated that he felt another meeting would be valuable if the Third Consultative Meeting was going to be held after 1963.[9] Argentina was obviously concerned about intergovernmental ties being maintained between the Consultative Meetings. This is an interesting position because Argentina was such an opponent of a secretariat for Antarctica, which would have solved the problem. By rejecting the idea of a secretariat while desiring close ties between the governments, Argentina was in an awkward position; this desire for a logistics meeting can best be understood as an attempt to address this paradox in Argentina's policy.

Opposite Argentina at the First Preparatory Meeting, Mr. Carr of Britain expresssed his government's opinion that another meeting on logistics would be unnecessary for several years. Before the debate heated up, South Africa and Australia closed the meeting by noting that time would be needed to absorb the data from the Boulder symposium and that it would be best to wait.[10]

The Second Preparatory Meeting of 4 April 1963 saw that little progress had been made in the month since the First Preparatory Meeting on the matter of technical issues. On logistics, the Australians reiterated their call for time to absorb SCAR's results. Norway and Chile expressed the view that communications, Australia, France and Britain announced that they had accepted the US invitation to the Washington Telecommunications Conference. Australia's Mr. Cumes asked that the agenda of the Conference be discussed at the next Preparatory Meeting.[11] There was nothing else said on either point.

At the Third Preparatory Meeting of 17 June 1963, almost nothing was accomplished on the Meetings of Experts. On logistics, the only shred of news was the French coming forward to support Australia's view that a new logistics meeting should be held a few years later on. The telecommunications issue was discussed only in so far as some delegations presented various agenda items for consideration.[12]

The Fourth Preparatory Meeting was held on 5 September 1963, and the Washington Conference on Telecommunications had been conducted in August. As a result, Belgium's van der Essen and Argentina's Guyer both asked that consideration of its report be included on the agenda of the Consultative Meeting. On logistics, nothing new occurred. Argentina remained adamant that another meeting on logistics be held, and Australia argued that to do so before 1965 would be a waste of time.[13]

This lack of progress on logistics continued at the Fifth Preparatory Meeting on 14 November 1963. However, the telecommunications issue proved more interesting, a more fertile ground for discussion. New Zealand's Mr. Piddington, Norway's Mr. Sondheim and Australia's Mr. Cumes announced that they had accepted the results (actually called Recommendations, but not to be confused with Recommendations from a Consultative Meeting) of the Washington Conference on Telecommunications. Mr. Cumes added that, in light of this acceptance, if the issue were on the agenda for the Consultative Meeting, it should only be for discussion, not for the purpose of passing new Recommendations. In response to inquiries from Mr. Philips of South Africa, Mr. Guyer of Argentina explained his country's insistence on including telecommunications on the Consultative Meeting's agenda stemmed from a belief that the Washington Telecommunications Conference was intended to report to the next Consultative Meeting, and its Recommendations would be adopted formally there.[14] This was the first hint that the relationship between Consultative Meetings and Meetings of Experts needed defining.

At the Sixth Preparatory Meeting 9 January 1964, only a few exchanges took place on the question of Meetings of Experts, telecommunications and logistics. The Japanese government's acceptance of the results of the Conference was announced by Mr. Tanida. Belgium's opinion was voiced by Mr. van der Essen that as a result of a Recommendation from Canberra, the Washington Conference on Telecommunications was held and therefore, it was up to a subsequent Consultative Meeting to approve the results. The UK disagreed with this position. Meanwhile, Argentina reiterated its desire for a logistics meeting.[15] Despite these statements, it did not yet seem that there was any significant difficulty in dealing with Expert's Meetings.

At the Seventh Preparatory Meeting, 5 March 1964, this perception changed. Although the discussion had originally covered whether the Consultative Meeting had to approve the report of a Meeting of Experts as a specific matter, i.e., did the Brussels Meeting have to approve the report from the Telecommunications Conference, the general problem in the relationship was recognized. Although the point was put on the table with broad support, Australia and the US had reservations about the idea, namely that it would establish rules for too rigid to make various Meetings of Experts worthwhile.[16]

The first real discussion of the relationship between Consultative Meetings and Meetings of Experts took place at the Eighth Preparatory Meeting, 3 April 1964. The US stated that the American government did not concur with the belief, held by many other governments, that Meetings of Experts, their reports and their Recommendations were on a par with Consultative Meetings. Mr. Cumes of Australia commented that Article IX of the Treaty was very unclear on the question and that the Consultative Powers needed to resolve the issue. In almost the same breath, he wondered if a simple exchange of views on the relationship would be best at the Third Consultative Meeting rather than issuing a Recommendation. South Africa and the UK echoed the sentiment that the question was important and had to be settled. The Chileans, represented by Mr. Pinochet de la Barra and Mr. Rodrigues, differed with the US suggestion that Meetings of Experts were somehow different from Consultative Meetings; a Recommendation was a Recommendation in Chilean eyes. Sensing the division's depth, South Africa's Mr. Philips noted that an exchange of views would be preferable. After a word in favor of talks from the British and the Japanese, the question was placed on the agenda for the Third Consultative Meeting.[17] It was agenda item eight, separate from the report of the telecommunications meeting (item

2) and the logistics symposium (item 12).[18]

At the Brussels Meeting itself, the logistics question saw little change in opinions since the Preparatory Meetings. Argentina repeated its arguments that the Boulder Symposium was not a substitute for an inter-governmental meeting as demanded by Recommendations from Canberra and Buenos Aires. Therefore, Argentina demanded that a date for an inter-governmental conference be set. The US strongly argued against this proposal fearing that a system of expensive logistical coopera- tion would result from it. Many draft proposals and long debates tried to bridge the gap. In the end, Recommendation III-III merely calls for the consideration of a logistical meeting at the next Consultative Meeting, embodying the US position by delaying the issue for two years.[19]

On telecommunications, there was a brief debate. Because some governments wanted a veto over any technical arrangements with financial implications, Recommendation III-V merely put the report of the Washington Conference on Telecommunications on the agenda for the next Consultative Meeting.[20]

As a direct result of the telecommunications debate, the Meeting addressed the relationship between Consultative Meetings and Meetings of Experts. South Africa and the UK held the belief that a distinction needed to be drawn between Consultative Meetings and "technical meetings." It was even suggested that technical symposia report to Consultative Meetings and not directly to governments. In effect, this would have made the Meetings of Experts subordinate to Consultative Meetings and would have given them the same standing as the working group that drafted the working paper on conservation. It also looked like an ersatz secretariat. Given that South Africa and Britain supported both the secretariat and this view on Meetings of Experts, an interpretation along these lines is not without some circumstantial support. For its part, the US disagreed, arguing that the stage had not yet been reached whereat distinctions should be made.[21] Given America's views from the Eighth Preparatory Meeting, that Meetings of Experts were not equal to Consultative Meetings, this seems to represent a change in sentiment.

If the American position was in opposition to that of Britain and South Africa, it was nothing compared to Australia's extreme stand. In the Australian view, there was no formalization of Meetings under the Treaty and there should be no Recommendation issued on the matter. The Australian position does cast some doubts as to whether this is a secretariat by the back-door. As a proponent of a secretariat, Australia's view here would be inconsistent if the intention of subordinating Meetings of Experts to Consultative Meetings was to establish a sort of secretariat. The final state to enter debate was Chile, which maintained that Consultative Meetings were distinct from Meetings of Experts. Chile argued that the latter had no standing under the Treaty whereas the former was established by provision of the Treaty. As a further point, it should be noted that Santiago, Chile had been selected for the next Meeting, and the impression of some delegations was that the Chileans feared that the Santiago Meeting would be a technical symposium rather than a prestigious Consultative Meeting.[22] With these deep divisions, the matter was put on the agenda for the Fourth Consultative Meeting under Recommendation III-VI and no other action was taken in Brussels.

When the Santiago Preparatory Meeting convened in September 1966, the delegates still had to address the issue of the Washington Telecommunications Conference, the proposals for a logistical Meeting of Experts and the relationship between Meetings of Experts and the Consultative Meetings. At the request of the Americans, the last point was discussed first; the reason being that if this point could be settled, tackling the other two would be made easier. Although the Preparatory Meeting would only decide what went on the agenda, if the matter were not inscripted on the agenda, it would affect discussions on the other two by its absence.

Accordingly, the views on the nature of Meetings of Experts opened the Preparatory Meeting. The United States stated its opinion that these conferences were completely consistent with Article IX of the Treaty but felt that they should not necessarily pass Recommendations, and if they were to do so, those Recommendations would not be binding on the governments. In concurring, the United Kingdom divided Meetings of Experts into two distinct classes: those called to reach agreement on technical matters and those called for the exchange of information on technical problems. Further, the UK felt it inappropriate to allow non-Consultative Powers to attent the second class in any capacity. To insure that this distinction remained, the Meetings of Experts should have definite goals and a firm agenda.[23] South Africa and Japan supported the British ideas, but Australia and Argentina took the view that there could be but one kind of meeting under Article IX. In private the Australians admitted to their American counterparts that this position was too extreme. Despite the disagreement, or perhaps because of it, the item was put on the agenda without reservation.[24]

At every Consultative Meeting since Canberra, Argentina, Australia and Chile had supported an inter-governmental meeting on logistics. In Santiago, this trio again sought to arrange a meeting. Argentina, arguing that much had changed since the Boulder symposium in 1962, felt a Meeting of Experts on logistics should be held in 1967 or 1968. Chile took this even further in adding a proposal for an annual, or semi-annual report on logistics to be published by SCAR.[25] Opposition to this came chiefly from the US and the UK. While not opposed to the idea of a Meeting of Experts, the UK believed it was unnecessary. If a majority of states wanted a meeting on logistics, the US would accept it but cautioned that SCAR's symposium should be considered to avoid any duplication of effort.[26] South Africa and Britain echoed this warning citing their respective financial worries. Japan, however, felt a technical discussion would fit in well with the Fifth Consultative Meeting. The French, probable hosts of the Fifth Consultative Meeting, opposed a Meeting of Experts and refused to consider hosting it, but they did not object to the inclusion of the item on the agenda.[27] It seems France, like Chile in 1964, feared it would host a less prestigious, technical meeting as opposed to a full-fledged Consultative Meeting. In addition, this demonstrates that although the diplomats had separated the question of telecommunications and logistics from the role of Meetings of Experts on paper, they still put them together in their comments.

Consideration of the Washington Telecommunications Conference was far less contentious. Belgium, Norway and the USSR voiced no objections to discussing the matter, although Belgium was of the opinion that the present arrangements for Antarctic telecommunications were adequate. Britain also favored discussing the meeting's report and brought the World Meteorological Organization's interest in the question to the attention of other delegations. The WMO's Executive Committee had expressed its concern over the delays in reporting meteorological measurements in Antarctica. The UK, the US, Argentina, Chile and South Africa all supported discussion of the specific problems of weather measurements but were concerned on how to get it on the agenda. Reflecting how different the Santiago preparations were from those for Brussels, Australia merely proposed that it be inserted under "other business". In that way, it was unanimously adopted.[28] In Brussels, this would have resulted in debate and the addition of another agenda item, with all the quibbling over terms and scope that that entailed.

At the Fourth Consultative Meeting, the discussion of technical issues started with the role of Meetings of Experts. The US proposed a Recommendation allowing Meetings of Experts to be held as needed. They would be attended by the Consultative Powers; they would have a set agenda with established objectives; they were not required to issue Recommendations; they would report to the individual governments of the participating countries; and any formal agreement would be placed on the agenda of the next Consulatative Meeting.[29] Chile, Japan, South Africa and the UK all supported the proposal. When New Zealand and France questioned who would convene the Meeting of Experts, the US responded that the Consultative Meeting would have that authority, thereby establishing the supremacy of the Consultative Meeting. The Belgians and Australians favored more emphasis being placed on Meetings of Experts that merely exchanged information as opposed to solving technical problems. In addition, the Australian Representative suggested that if the Meetings of Experts could not make binding Recommendations, it would be more appropriate for the experts to find their own frames of reference rather than having it established by the Consultative Meeting. Argentina and the Soviet Union agreed with the spirit of the proposal, but they preferred that the Meeting of Experts report back to a Consultative Meeting.[30] Recommendation IV-24 is a compromise; Meetings of Experts are to be called at Consultative Meetings or by diplomatic channels, are to be attended by representatives of the Concultative Powers and approved observers, to have the host nation circulate the final report and to have the report submitted to the next Consultative Meeting, unless otherwise agreed.

Although logistics and telecommunications continued to be significant issues in future Consultative Meetings, the real structural issue had been dealt with by Recommendation IV-24. Meetings of Experts were to be considered subordinate to Consultative Meetings. The diplomats would continue to hold a monopoly on decision-making in Antarctica. This is not to say that the scientific community had lost its influence in Antarctic politics. After all, Recommendations IV-1 to IV-17 establishing SPAs and SPSs were taken from SCAR's report on the matter, and in the view of the American delegation the unanimity of scientists in the SCAR report carried a lot of weight with the delegations.[31] This was at the same Consultative Meeting that passed Recommendation IV-24 making Meetings of Experts subordinate to Consultative Meetings. The significance of this is that it established the demarcation of responsibility between diplomats and scientists. While the technical people were allowed to recommend actions, the decision-makers would have the final say. When the question was purely technical, the diplomats would defer to their technical experts. However, if issues of a technical nature threatened to spill-over into financial or territorial matters, to name but two, the diplomats wanted to make certain that they had control over the situation.

NOTES

[1]National Science Foundation, "Trip Report to the First Consultative Meeting", p. 3.

[2]United States, Department of State, "Draft Position Paper on Radio Communications in Antarctica", RG 307, Box 29, File 102.1.1.

[3]National Science Foundation, "Trip Report to the First Consultative Meeting", p 4.

[4]Recommendation I-XI.

[5]United States Navy, "Memo for the Record", p. 2.

[6]National Science Foundation, "Trip Report to the Second Consultative Meeting", p. 2.

[7]United States Navy, "Memo for the Record", p. 3.

[8]*Ibid.*

[9]Department of State, Division of Language Services, "Minutes of the First Meeting in Preparation..." *passim.*

[10]*Ibid.*

[11]Department of State, "Minutes of the Second Meeting in Preparation ...", p. 2.

[12]Department of State, "Procès-Verbal de la Troisième Réunion Préparatoire ...", pp. 4-5.

[13]Department of State, Division of Language Services, "Minutes of the Fourth Meeting in Preparation ...", p. 9.

[14]Department of State, "Procès-Verbal de la 5ème Réunion Préparatoire ...", pp. 5-7.

[15]Department of State, "Procès-Verbal de la 6ème Réunion Préparatoire ...", pp. 5-6.

[16]Department of State, "Procès-Verbal de la 7ème Réunion Préparatoire ...", pp. 4-5.

[17]Department of State, "Procès-Verbal de la 8ème Réunion Préparatoire ...", p. 2.

[18]United States, Department of State, "Points Inscrits a L'Ordre du Jour de la 3ème Réunion Consultative de Bruxelles", Enclosure Two to Air- gram A-1095, US Embassy Brussels to Department of State Washington, May 1964, RG 307, Box 18, File 102D.

[19]Department of State, "Report of the US Delegation to the Third Consultative Meeting ...", p. 3. Since the source is American, one may take the alleged victory of the American position with a grain of salt. The author's reading of the situation differs with the official American assess- ment of Recommendation III-III.

[20]Ibid., p. 4.

[21]Ibid., p. 5.

[22]Ibid.

[23]Department of State, "Preparatory Delegation Report," Draft Version, p. 1.

[24]Ibid.

[25]Ibid.

[26]United States, Department of State, "Position Paper for the Fourth Consultative Meeting: Meeting of Experts on Logistics," Draft Version, 19 May 1966, RG 307, Box 18, File 102D.

[27]Department of State, "Preparatory Delegation Report", pp. 2-3.

[28]Ibid., p. 3.

[29]United States, Department of State, "Position Paper for the Fourth Consultative Meeting: Meetings of Experts", 26 October 1966, RG 313, Box 80, File 2A112.

[30]United States, Department of State, "Report of the US Delegation to the Fourth Consultative Meeting: Meetings of Experts", RG 307, Box 19, File 102D.

[31]See previous Chapter.

CHAPTER VII
ROLE OF SCAR

Unlike the previous issues dealt with by the first Consultative Meetings, the role of SCAR is more difficult to examine because it was settled in theory at the Canberra Meeting, but in practice, the question remained unresolved. Therefore, a problem arose due to the official status of SCAR and its practical status clashing.

That SCAR should play a role in the Antarctic System was inevitable. In the American proposals during the 1940s, a scientific body was envisioned that would address the technical issues that arose in the Antarctic. Although the eventual agreement achieved in 1959 differs from these proposals, the support from a technical body of some sort was necessary by the very nature of human activity in Antarctica. With research as its primary industry, Antarctica would require a technical organization to carry out the numerous coordinating functions that would exist.

In addition, during the IGY, this coordinating function was demonstrated to be of benefit. Since SCAR was the body designed to facilitate research in the Antarctic in the IGY/IGC, it had already established itself in the role of a technical support organization. However, in the Antarctic Treaty, there is no mention of SCAR. The relationship of the Treaty to SCAR had to be established as did its functioning under the agreement.

The first mention of SCAR as a part of the Antarctic System came as part of the first issue addressed at the Canberra Meeting. On the matter of the exchange of scientific plans and future programs, New Zealand proposed a Recommendation that urged governments to make such information available to other concerned governments through SCAR and other channels. This idea had the support of the US Representative, in part because it was already US policy to do so, and in part because this was already established practice for many Consultative Powers.[1] Recommendation I-I simply formalizes this exchange by giving SCAR the role of an information clearing house. As the purpose of SCAR during the IGY was essentially that of a body that carried out liaison activities between the national IGY committees, this is not a significant change. What is important is that the System formally gave recognition to SCAR's activities.

Also on the agenda of the First Consultative Meeting was an item concerning the relations between the Consultative Powers and SCAR. These discussions were perhaps the most heated of all the talks in Canberra. At the interim meetings in Washington, numerous scientists voiced their concerns about SCAR's future. The International Council of Scientific Unions, which established SCAR for the IGY,[2] is a non-governmental body. Hence the ICSU and its component parts are independent of direct governmental controls. In fact, during the IGY the national committees were the go-betweens for SCAR and the participating governments. In Canberra, the British favored making SCAR the official implementor of Article III of the Treaty, i.e., giving SCAR official standing to oversee the exchange of plans, personnel and scientific data as well as carrying on cooperative relations with the UN and other international bodies.[3] This would have established SCAR as a governmental organization and made it the *de facto* bureaucracy for the Antarctic.

Opposition to this came from the US, which preferred inter-governmental cooperation.[4] In Canberra, the Americans made three proposals encouraging governments to use SCAR in their exchange of data, but these were rejected by Argentina, Belgium, Chile and France. A fourth, which added wording on "other arrangements" for the exchange, overcame the objections of those four states only to be rejected by the UK, which desired SCAR to be the sole channel for data exchanges. The discussions went on for several days, but the compromise in Recommendation I-IV did not vary greatly from the first three American proposals.[5] Under the compromise, SCAR remained an independent, non-governmental body and continued governmental contacts with SCAR were encouraged. It is important to note that ties to other international organizations are in the following Recommendation, I-V. The purpose of this was to recognize SCAR by name. In the case of the Americans, it was seen as important to keep UN specialized agencies at arm's length due to the unanimity rules in force there. The American preference for keeping SCAR involved and non-governmental was because if a change were made, SCAR would be less free to act and would be more politicized.[6]

It would appear from this that the part SCAR was to play was settled by the provisions in Recommendation I-IV. However, the Recommendation is vague, especially on encouraging continued governmental contact with SCAR. As part of a compromise in diplomacy, it was probably left vague purposely. Yet that does not alter the fact that loosely worded agreements frequently run into a situation that requires more precision.

The first instance of this came at the Buenos Aires Meeting when it came time to discuss the exchange of logistical information. Australia and Argentina backed a plan to hold meetings on this matter in the latter half of 1963 under the aegis of the Consultative Powers despite the fact that SCAR was holding its own symposium on the topic in August 1962.[7] Although the debate then moved onto other aspects of the proposal, it suggests that at least Argentina and Australia were of the opinion that SCAR was not part of the Antarctic System. Despite the fact that SCAR would probably exhaust the subject,[8] they felt that the Consultative Powers were under some obligation to hold their own symposium or meeting to address the issue.

At the First Preparatory Meeting for the Brussels Consultative Meeting, the issue arose again under the discussion of a logistics meeting. The delegations were divided into two camps, the first holding that logistics were a governmental responsibility, and thus requiring governmental action, and the second believing that SCAR's symposium had done all the work necessary.[9] This division resulted in part from an unclear view of

SCAR's status in the System. Those states that believed it was not a real appendage of the System, e.g., Argentina, desired a governmental logistics meeting. Those that believed SCAR was an independent but related organization felt that a further meeting would be redundant.

At the Second Preparatory Meeting, this division persisted. Norway and Chile's statements that a further meeting would be useless demonstrated their view as to SCAR's role. Australia's desire for time to absorb the results of SCAR's symposium hints at a change of heart by the Australians at a practical level only.[10] It seems that although in favor of a logistics meeting held by the governments, Australia felt that SCAR had exhausted the field and adoption of its results would settle the matter in practical terms. A meeting for the sake of holding a meeting seems to have sat badly with them.

The divergent views on SCAR's role emerged again at the Third Preparatory Meeting as the Powers discussed the draft agreements on conservation. The Soviets' amendment to Britain's draft called for replacing "Consultative Meeting" with "SCAR". As mentioned in the examination of conservation issues,[11] this does not tell the student of the System very much. However, it is clear from this that the Soviets were acting under the impression that SCAR was part of the System; so much so in fact, that they felt comfortable replacing certain functions of the Consultative Meetings with action by SCAR. The contrast between this and Argentina's view derived from the logistics debates previous shows how unclear SCAR's role was in the thinking of the Consultative Powers.

At the Fourth Preparatory Meeting, the first matter of business was the exchange of views on a request by the World Meteorological Organization that the Consultative Powers establish a permanent committee on Antarctic meteorology. Although Australia, New Zealand, France, Japan, South Africa and Belgium favored the idea, many states reserved their position until after SCAR's meeting, held in the same month, September 1963, had discussed the matter.[12] From this, one may safely deduce that several of the Consultative Powers were using SCAR as a think tank, having it do the technical work on meteorology rather than setting up a committee themselves. Their reservations may probably be seen best as deferring to the experts, but it is clear that by experts, at least in the field of technical support, they meant SCAR.

At the Eighth Preparatory Meeting, this position on SCAR is reiterated. As part of their conservation proposals, the British wanted SCAR to issue tri-annual reports on Antarctic flora and fauna.[13] Since the British were proponents in Canberra of giving SCAR the oversight responsibilities for Article III, this is not a surprise. Howver, Recommendation I-IV does not call for this sort of action by SCAR. Continued contacts by the governments seems to fall short of having SCAR publish reports in support of the conservation activities by the Consultative Powers.

At the Brussels Consultative Meeting itself, Argentina made it clear that it did not see SCAR in quite the same light as the British or the Soviets. In discussing the need for an intergovernmental logistics meeting, the Argentinian Representative stressed that he did not think a SCAR symposium was a substitute for the sort of meeting he proposed. By that, SCAR was not able to take the place of a meeting under the Consultative Powers under any circumstances; SCAR was not part of the Treaty apparatus and should not be allowed a role it was not given.[14]

In the preamble of the Agreed Measures, the only reference to SCAR comes in terms that suggest SCAR is distinct from the machinery of the Antarctic Treaty. "Having particular regard to the conservation principles developed by the Scientific Committee on Antarctic Research ..." is the only time SCAR is mentioned in the Agreed Measures.[15] In this, the Argentine view of SCAR seemed to carry the day over the British or Soviet view.

Despite that, the Consultative Powers took an almost diametrically opposed tone in Recommendation III-X. This essentially dealt with gathering more data on the Antarctic ecosystem to implement the Agreed Measures with more precision. Therefore, SCAR was encouraged to promote research on this point, and as per Britain's proposal, it was to issue reports on Antarctic flora and fauna. While this is not a command, "encourage" was the word used in the actual text, it does appear that SCAR is being instructed by the Consultative Powers to act. Granted that SCAR's function under Recommendation I-IV was to assist in the exchange of data, this is the first instance of SCAR being "encouraged" to handle a particular sort of data. In the American view, and significantly so, there was no problem in adopting these conservation Recommendations so long as there was no implication that SCAR was "an agent of the Consultative Meetings."[16] Yet, it would appear that Recommendation III-X implies just that.

At the Santiago Preparatory Meeting, SCAR arose again in discussion of a logistical meeting. Although the debate stuck to the desirability of a meeting of this kind, Chile did propose that an annual or semi-annual report on logistics be published by SCAR.[17] This is, of course, merely a logical extension of the conservation reports Britain pushed through the Third Consultative Meeting. However, logistical data are far less scientific in nature than data on conservation. By the Chilean proposal, SCAR would become a primarily scientific, rather than exclusively scientific, organization. Although the proposal did not generate much support, it is important to note the kinds of things the Consultative Powers were proposing to have SCAR do because it shows what they felt SCAR's position to be.

At the Santiago Consultative Meeting, the SCAR question arose in three different discussions. Given the ties between logistics as an issue and SCAR's role, it is hardly surprising that the matter arose again when the delegations addressed the proposed logistical conference. Additionally, when the technical annexes to the Agreed Measures came up for discussion, SCAR's role was called into question. Finally, it even arose in scheduling the Fifth Consultative Meeting.

In the discussion on a logistical conference, there was general support throughout the delegations that a clash between it and any SCAR meeting be avoided. Australia demarcated the boundary between the two by saying that a SCAR meeting would deal with scientific solutions to technical problems while a Meeting of Experts would handle the matters of political coordination.[18] This view received support from France, Argentina and Britain, but the US, concerned for SCAR's freedom, cautioned the delegates on presuming to dictate to SCAR.[19] The discussion then moved away from SCAR's position, but the important clash had been shown. Under Australia's proposal, an awkward scheme would exist of Consultative Meetings, Meetings of Experts and SCAR conferences. Because the relations between Meetings of Experts and the Consultative Meetings had not been settled, this is understandable but clearly undesirable. SCAR would be made an official member of the System responsible for, in addition to other things, scientific solutions to technical problems. This function would then call into question the exis- tence of Meetings of Experts because as it was finally agreed, Consultative Meetings would handle the political side of technical issues. Meetings of Experts would then merely replicate SCAR's actions.

When the delegates discussed the annexes to the Agreed Measures, SCAR's influence in the scientific field was demonstrated. The technical annexes were the parts of the Agreed Measures establishing Specially Protected Areas (SPAs) and Specially Protected Species (SPSs). Just prior to the Santiago Meeting, SCAR had finished a report on these, suggesting which places and animals should be declared SPAs and SPSs. The unani- mous agreement of the scientists of SCAR greatly influenced the dele- gates. Those areas and species suggested by SCAR received special status in the technical annexes.[20]

As a tangential issue for the delegates, but a significant one here, this led to the discussion of the status of SCAR papers at the Consultative Meetings. Both Chile and the USSR favored their use as conference documents, giving them the status as proposed Recommendations and proposed agreement drafts. The US opposed this, trying to keep SCAR independent. A compromise resulted in SCAR documents being referred to but given no official standing.[21] Nothing demonstrates the divisions on SCAR's role as well as this.

As its final point of business, the Fourth Consultative Meeting had to decide when and where to meet the next time. The French had offered to host the Fifth Consultative Meeting, and this was accepted. Privately, the delegates agreed to try to keep the Paris Meeting from conflicting with a SCAR congress.[22] The reasons for this are mainly practical: a conflict might take a scientific advisor or two away from a delegation to the Paris Meeting, it might cause many topics to be deferred, and SCAR might produce some important work that the Paris Meeting should address. However, it is also obvious that SCAR was becoming a factor in the plans of the Consultative Powers, perhaps beyond the extent of Recommendation I-IV.

In preparation for the Paris Meeting, this concern for the SCAR congress continued. As its first order of business, the First Preparatory Meeting had to settle on a date for the Fifth Consultative Meeting. When the French offered 15 October 1968 as a date, the US and UK pointed out that that would keep the Consultative Powers from addressing the results of the SCAR congress. The UK stated that SCAR would be meeting until 4 August and that two months would be required to absorb the information. The opening of the Fifth Consultative Meeting was delayed, therefore, until 18 November 1968.[23] SCAR was such a part of the System by this stage, despite its legal independence, that it was a factor for the Consultative Powers in deciding when to meet.

This was further demonstrated at the Fourth Preparatory Meeting held in Paris. When the delegates reached other business on the agenda, Australia's representative suggested that conflicts between Consultative Meetings and SCAR meetings should be prevented. It was proposed that they be held in alternate years, but that some flexibility should exist regarding Consultative Meetings.[24] It might be reading too much into the proposal to suggest that the Australians meant that flexibility not be allowed for SCAR's meetings, but in even proposing it, SCAR is tied even more closely to the Treaty apparatus. It would appear that the Australians received considerable support for their idea because the "Coordination of SCAR's General Meetings and Consultative Meetings" was item 11 on the agenda for Paris.[25]

In Paris, there were two occasions where SCAR had some impact on discussions. The first was in the discussion of pelagic sealing. The second, logically, was in the debate on coordinating SCAR meetings and Consultative Meetings.

In the case of pelagic sealing, Britain circulated the proposals set out in SCAR's general meeting. This was entirely in line with the agreement that SCAR documents would be referred to without official standing for Santiago. However, it is significant that this was actually done. SCAR's proposals put SCAR in the position of "encouraging" the Consultative Powers to act. Moreover, during the discussions, the Soviets insisted that SCAR's proposals be adopted verbatim.[26] Clearly, SCAR's opinion had come to count for a great deal in the deliberations of the Consultative Powers.

When the delegates debated the coordination of SCAR meetings and Consultative Meetings, the French suggested that they be held in alternate years, echoing Australia's early proposal. The Japanese, however, pointed out that that would be impossible because SCAR's next meeting and the Sixth Consultative Meeting in Tokyo had already been set for 1970. In addition, the French proposal, really SCAR circular 218, offended some Representatives by its tone.[27] The US, for its part, favored avoiding any rigid formula.[28] In the end, the Japanese invitation to meet in Tokyo in 1970 was formally accepted as Recommendation V-9, and Belgium led a call for SCAR to change the date of its planned meeting.[29] Obviously, this is a case of the Consultative Powers pressuring SCAR, and there seems to have been no effort to protect SCAR's independence. Certainly, no reservations about it are mentioned. The question of coordinating the various meetings demonstrates that SCAR, despite the statements to the contrary, had become a functioning part of the Antarctic System.

SCAR's technical support role in the Antarctic System has, if anything, grown over the years. Recommendations continue to be passed "encouraging", "requesting" or "suggesting" that SCAR act in one way or another, e.g. Recommendations VI-5, VII-1, VIII-3, IX-1, X-1, etc. Often, it is phased that SCAR shall be contacted by way of the national committees to pursue these ends, but this is merely paying lip-service to SCAR's legal status under the Treaty. SCAR, in practice, is the technical support body of the Treaty.

Moreover, in the cases of the Treaty on Pelagic Sealing and the Convention on the Conservation of Marine Living Resources, SCAR is given legal status as an arm of each. Because these are separate from the Treaty, SCAR's independence is preserved to a degree. However, as these documents are supportive of the Antarctic Treaty and grew out of the Consultative Meetings, they seem to put SCAR clearly in the position of being part of the System as a whole. In the instance of the sealing agreement, SCAR is designated as the official scientific advisory body; Articles 4, 5, 6 and technical annexes 6 and 7 mention SCAR by name in enumeration of duties and information exchanges. As for the broader Convention on Conservation of Antarctic Marine Living Resources, the machinery of the agreement is set up differently, but the bodies established are instructed to establish a cooperative working relationship with SCAR under Article XXIII.[30]

Therefore, despite the provisions of Recommendation I-IV, SCAR has become the central scientific support organization for the Consultative Powers and serves a vital function for the Antarctic System. Its independence is a matter for debate, but the working relationship between the Consultative Meetings and SCAR has had its soundness proved. Although the legal distinctions remain vague, the important factor is that SCAR is backing up the Treaty and supporting agreements.

NOTES

[1]United States, Department of State, "Draft Position Paper on the Exchange of Information on Scientific Programs," RG 307, Box 29, File 102.1.1.

[2]See Chapter III.

[3]National Science Foundation, "Trip Report to the First Consultative Meeting," p. 2.

[4]United States, Department of State, "Draft Position Paper on Relations with SCAR," RG 307, Box 29, File 102.1.1.

[5]National Science Foundation, "Trip Report to the First Consultative Meeting," p. 2.

[6]*Ibid.*, p. 3.

[7]National Science Foundation, "Trip Report to the Second Consultative Meeting," p. 2. See also Chapter V.

[8]United States Navy, "Memo for the Record," p. 3.

[9]Department of State, Division of Language Services, "Minutes of the First Meeting in Preparation ...", *passim*. See also Chapter VI.

[10]Department of State, "Minutes of the Second Meeting in Preparation ...", p. 2.

[11]Department of State, "Procès-Verbal de la Troisième Réunion Préparatoire ...", p. 2.

[12]Department of State, Division of Language Services, "Minutes of the Fourth Meeting in Preparation ...", pp. 2-5.

[13]Department of State, "Procès-Verbal de la 8ème Réunion Préparatoire ...", p. 6.

[14]Department of State, "Report of the US Delegation to the Third Consultative Meeting," p. 4.

[15]Preamble to the Agreed Measures.

[16]Department of State, "Report of the US Delegation to the Third Consultative Meeting," p. 8.

[17]Department of State, "Preparatory Delegation Report," Draft Version, p. 1.

[18]See Chapter VI.

[19]Department of State, "Report of the US Delegation to the Fourth Consultative Meeting: Meeting of Experts on Logistics."

[20]Department of State, "Report of the US Delegation to the Fourth Consultative Meeting: Annexes to the Agreed Measures ...", pp. 1-2.

[21]*Ibid.*, pp. 2-3.

[22]United States, Department of State, "Report of the US Delegation to the Fourth Consultative Meeting: Place and Date of Next Meeting," RG 307, Box 19, File 102D.

[23]Department of State, "Minutes of the First Preparatory Meeting for the Fifth Consultative Meeting," p. 1.

[24]Department of State, "Minutes of the Fourth Preparatory Meeting for the Fifth Consultative Meeting."

[25]Department of State, "Report ... Fifth Consultative Meeting."

[26]*Ibid.*, p. 6.

[27]*Ibid.*, p. 19.

[28]United States, Department of State, "Position Paper on the Coordination of SCAR General Meetings and Consultative Meetings," RG 307, Box 20, File 102D.

[29]Department of State, "Report ... Fifth Consultative Meeting."

[30]For a detailed study of the Convention on the Conservation of Antarctic Marine Living Resources, see F. M. Auburn, *Antarctic Law and Politics*, pp. 211-16, and for the text of the agreement, pp. 319-35.

CHAPTER VIII
DUTIES OF ACCEDING STATES

The purpose of the Consultative Meetings is, of course, to facilitate in implementation of the terms of the Treaty. The Consultative Powers make Recommendations that have the force of executive agreements in order to aid in the execution of the Treaty. There is, however, a legal difficulty in this approach to the problems of the Antarctic, and like all legal issues it has a political side to it.

International law is composed of state custom, i.e., the practice of states as evidence of a code of conduct by nations, and contractual law. In the case of the Antarctic, it is clear that only contractual law is of concern. Although such concepts of customary law as *uti possidetis juris* influence the issue of territorial sovereignty, the Treaty itself is a pact between governments and therefore, it and its supporting arrangements are contractual in nature. The key principle in contractual international law is that no state is bound or can be bound to an arrangement without its consent. In other words, until a state expresses its willingness to obey a given rule, it cannot be forced to do so.

In the Antarctic System, a problem arises because of the relationship of acceding states and the Recommendations in force prior to that state's accession. By acceding, the state has accepted the terms of the Treaty, but the Recommendations are not part of the Treaty itself; they are executive agreements in support of it. It is possible, therefore, for a state to accede to the Treaty under Article XIII while refusing to accept any Recommendation it pleases. Because these agreements are the cornerstone of the Treaty, this situation has the potential to undermine the entire System. After all, what benefit is there for the original signatories to agree on measures for conservation, to cite but one example, if new parties to the Treaty refuse to accept them and cannot be compelled to comply?

This particular issue, the duties of acceding states with regard to existing Recommendations, did not arise until the preparations for the Third Consultative Meeting in Brussels. This is entirely understandable because the Consultative Powers did not establish the informal rule that each Consultative Meeting would produce Recommendations that would further the aims of the Treaty until after the first couple of Consultative Meetings. By 1964, though, it was apparent that something would have to be done to prevent the Treaty from being undermined by new parties to the agreement.

At the Sixth Preparatory Meeting in Brussels, as its final point of business, the Belgian delegate Mr. van der Essen, raised the issue; if an acceding state becomes a Contracting Party to the Treaty after a given Recommendation enters into force, is that state bound by the Recommendation in question?   To solve the problem, the Belgian government proposed amending the Treaty, specifically Article XIII, so that acceding states become Contracting Parties "on condition that they accept also the Recommendations of the Consultative Meetings, approved in conformity with the provisions of Article IX paragraph 4 and in force at the moment of accession."[1]   The proposing delegate acknowledged that this would discourage states from accepting the Treaty, no matter how much they supported its principles, if they were thereby bound to unacceptable Recommendations.   As an alternative, Mr. van der Essen suggested an amendment to Article IX paragraph 2, adding to the provisions on attaining Consultative status the following: "[Consultative status is granted to states] ... on condition of having accepted the Recommendations of the Consultative Meetings approved prior to the moment of participation."[2]

The Belgian intent was obviously to overcome the problem of acceding states.   However, it opened up a far greater threat to the Treaty by the manner in which it tried to solve the problem.   This is not to belittle the proposals, and it cannot be denied that a situation in which an acceding state could opt out of an undesirable Recommendation with impunity was a significant threat.   Yet by amending the Treaty to force acceding states to accept all previous Recommendations (setting aside for the moment the legal problems of ratification and the discouragement it would be to accession), the Belgian proposals could have activated Article XII paragraph 1 section B whereby states can withdraw from the Treaty by not ratifying an amendment.   The Belgian proposals would, indeed, close the existing loop-hole, but they also could kill the Treaty.   This was not even three years after the Treaty entered into force.   The Sixth Preparatory Meeting closed before much discussion of the amendment proposals could occur.

At the Seventh Preparatory Meeting in Brussels, Belgium again took the lead in the discussion.   The Belgian position held that an amendment to the Treaty would offer the best hope of solving the problem of acceding states.   Despite that, an alternative was offered by Mr. van der Essen, specifically a Recommendation that would interpret Article IX paragraph 2, the granting of Consultative status, so as to close the existing loop-hole. That provision states that countries demonstrating an interest in Antarctica by scientific research can be made Consultative Powers.   The Belgian Recommendation would interpret "interest" broadly so that acceptance of all previous Recommendations would be included in demonstrating interest in Antarctica.[3]

Although this might be stretching the intent of the Treaty's terms, it is obvious that the Belgian government was trying to solve the issue.   It would appear that they had abandoned the idea of amending Article XIII to require all acceding states to accept Recommendations in force.   Instead, the proposals would bind those seeking Consultative status, i.e., those actively engaged in various pursuits in Antarctica.   Since acceding states are not always active on the continent, e.g., Czechoslovakia, binding them was far less important than getting active states, potential Consultative Powers, to accept the Recommendations already in effect.   There is, however, a political problem with this, whether by amending the Treaty or by a Recommendation interpreting "interest" broadly, and that is the discouragement this would be to a state seeking Consultative status. At the Sixth Preparatory Meeting, the Belgians had noted that amendment of Article XIII might be a discouragement to accede to the Treaty. The same applies, albeit to a more limited number of states, here. Hypothetically, though, a state may be active in Antarctica and eligible for Consultative status by the terms of the Treaty but it may decline to seek full participation at the Consultative Meetings because of an unacceptable Recommendation. If a state in this position should refuse to join the Consultative club and ignore the offensive Recommendation, the Treaty would be in serious trouble. Although the Belgian proposals were excellent efforts, they did not completely put the issue to rest.

Until the Eighth Preparatory Meeting, the Belgians seemed to have to carry the debate on by themselves. However, at the Eighth Preparatory Meeting, South Africa voiced its support of Belgium's intention to amend the Treaty. The UK and Australia felt that the Belgian proposal did not go far enough, perhaps for the reasons cited above. However, the French captured the spirit of the discussion by calling the need to get acceding states to accept Recommendations in force "indispensible." Although the Americans felt it would be reasonable to discuss the matter, no Recommendation should come from it. The reasoning behind this is unfathomable. Sensing that the real concern was binding states active in Antarctica, Belgium proposed it be put on the agenda as "application of Article IX paragraph 2," which was approved.[4] Thus, only states seeking Consultative status would be affected.

At the Brussels Consultative Meeting, the Consultative Powers started the debate on the duties of acceding states with a formal proposal by the Belgian Representative to amend the Treaty to make all Recommendations binding on all Contracting Parties. Technically, this would appear to be out of order, as such an amendment would affect Article XIII and not Article IX as on the agenda. However, there was no need for this to be ruled out of order (interestingly, the Chairman of the Meeting was the Belgian Representative who also proposed the idea, so this could only be done by appealing to the other delegations) because of the general opposition to amending the Treaty.[5] Apparently, the delegates felt that amendment was a more serious threat to the System than were any potential, recalcitrant new-comers.

To counter the Belgian proposals, Australia's delegation advanced a proposal urging Contracting Parties to accept the Recommendations in force. This would be in the form of a Recommendation. Some states felt that only those about to become Consultative Powers should be urged to accept them, while leaving the door open for others to do so.[6] This is more in line with the agenda, which specified Article IX paragraph 2. In any case, this particular view carried the day, the verb "urge" is used only for new Consultative Powers in Recommendation III-VII. Others are "invited to consider accepting" Recommendations in force.[7]

Quite clearly, this had no real effect on the issue. At best, it is a resolution expressing the sense of the delegations but no more. A state that strenuously objects to a particular Recommendation will not alter its view merely because it has been "urged" to do so. Although Recommendation III-VII addresses the difficulty, it does nothing to settle the matter.

Apparently, the Consultative Powers were aware of the ineffectiveness of Recommendation III-VII because the question arose again at the Preparatory Meeting in Santiago. Because the US had yet to approve Recommendation III-VII, and therefore, since it was not yet in force, the question arose of whether acceding states were bound by it.[8] If they were, then Recommendations III-VII weakened the language in the Treaty; if not, then the Treaty was strengthened by it. Britain maintained that acceding states were not bound by it, but Argentina maintained that the Treaty and the Recommendations were indivisible and therefore, acceding states were bound by it.[9] The Argentine position, while doubtful from a legal standpoint, prevented a split among the legal obligations of the Contracting Parties. If the British position prevailed, there could be states bound by all the Recommendations, some bound by a few and other bound by none. Given the gravity of the issue, the item was placed on the agenda by unanimous consent.[10]

Exactly what became of the question at the Santiago Meeting is uncertain. No Recommendation came out of it, and there seems to be little of significant change. Judging from the American position paper on the issue, Recommendation III-VII was adequate if it could be clarified.[11] Revision or clarification would, in the American opinion, have to: 1) require all acceding states to bind themselves to specific provisions of Recommendations, 2) show the close "organic" ties between the Treaty provisions and the Recommendations, and 3) imply that by accepting the Treaty the Recommendations have been accepted.[12] This seems to have been altered in inter-departmental discussions because of financial implications requisite in explicit acceptance of certain measures. In the end, the US position held that revision of Recommendation III-VII should: 1) urge acceding states that are active in the Antarctic to accept existing Recommendations, 2) invite other acceding parties to do likewise, 3) cite which Recommendations in particular should be accepted, 4) refer to Article X of the Treaty, whereby the Contracting Parties agree to undertake efforts to ensure no one acts in Antarctica contrary to the Treaty's provisions, and 5) have the depositary government, i.e., the American government, do the "urging."[13]

As part of the Final Report for the Santiago Meeting, there was an explanatory note on Recommendation III-VII. It did not have the same force or status as a Recommendation, but as part of the Final Report, it is an expression of the opinion of the Consultative Powers. This note enumerated five points regarding the duty of acceding states to accept the Recommendation:

1. *In becoming Parties to the Antarctic Treaty, States bind themselves to carry out its provisions and to uphold its purposes and principles;*

2. *Recommendations which become effective in accordance with Article IX of the Treaty are, in the terms of that Article, 'measures in furtherance of the principles and objectives of the Treaty';*

3. *Approved Recommendations are an essential part of the overall structure of cooperation established by the Treaty;*

4. *In pursuance of the principles and objectives of the Treaty there should be uniformity of practice in the activity of all Parties active in Antarctica; and*

5. *Approved Recommendations are to be viewed in the light of the obligations assumed by Contracting Parties under the Treaty and in particular Article X.*[14]

The essential points are 2 and 5. By defining Recommendations as the instruments of Articles IX and X, the Consultative Powers established that they had to be accepted as part of the Treaty itself. However, this is legally questionable. For obvious reasons, the Treaty itself was not going to be amended, but this explanatory note does not really do the job. A state could still accede and reject Recommendation III-VII and the explanatory note. It is difficult to see how this could be resolved, at least legally.

In the discussions on the exchange of information under Article VII paragraph 5, the Consultative Powers found that they had some influence to wield with regard to acceding states. The exchange of information could be extended only to Consultative States. However, a consensus emerged to extend it to acceding states. As only Argentina, Australia, Belgium and France were not supplying the data to them, a policy of such sharing was agreed, although there does seem to have been some grumbling by the Argentine delegate. Perhaps to make it a voluntary change of policy, the US, the UK and New Zealand successfully argued against codifying it in a Recommendation. In private talks with the Americans, the Argentine delegate noted that withholding such information from acceding states was one way to compel them to accept previously approved Recommendations.[15]

Although no codification of this has yet been approved, it does show a possible lever for the Consultative States to use against a state that fails to accept a Recommendation. Perhaps the greatest benefit to being a party to the Treaty is the exchange of data about Antarctic research. Only Consultative Powers or those in a position to request it generate any data about Antarctica as they are the only ones active there. They possess a monopoly on information. By denying a recalcitrant state access to the information, it is conceivable that the Consultative Powers could force, if not compliance, a change of some kind in the policy of the offending state.

Legally, the problem remains; a state that refuses to accept a rule cannot by the nature of international law, be held to it. Resolution of this is possible by amending the Treaty; then, any acceding state would accept the Recommendations as part of the terms of the Treaty. Because of the formula for terminating the Treaty that amendments can activate, though, that path was seen as impractical and undesirable. Instead, the

Consultative Powers adopted a doubtful Recommendation, III-VII, to settle the issue, and then, they clarified it. The real power, though, lies in their ability to deny data to a state. As yet, this has not been necessary, but perhaps it is adequate as a deterrent.

NOTES

[1]Department of State, "Procès-Verbal de la 6ème Réunion Préparatoire ...", p. 9. Author's Translation.

[2]*Ibid.*, p. 10. Author's Translation.

[3]Department of State, "Procès-Verbal de la 7ème Réunion Préparatoire ...", pp. 7-8.

[4]Department of State, "Procès-Verbal de la 8ème Réunion Préparatoire ...", pp. 4-5.

[5]Department of State, "Report ... Third Consultative Meeting ...", p. 5.

[6]*Ibid.*, p. 6.

[7]*Ibid.*

[8]Department of State, "Preparatory Delegation Report," p. 6. It is difficult to understand why this question arose. If it were not in force for the US due to American failure to approve it, then it could not be in force for an acceding state that had not. If an acceding state had accepted it, then it would be in force for that state because of its acceptance.

[9]*Ibid.*, p. 7.

[10]*Ibid.*

[11]United States, Department of State, "Position Paper for the Fourth Consultative Meeting: Recommendations of the Consultative Meetings," 27 October 1966, RG 313, Box 80, File 2A112.

[12]*Ibid.*

[13]*Ibid.*

[14]Antarctic Treaty, *Final Report of the Fourth Antarctic Consultative Meeting.* National Archives of the United States, Center for Polar Archives, Reference File.

[15]United States, Department of State, "Report of the US Delegation to the Fourth Consultative Meeting: Exchange of Information," Draft Version, RG 307, Box 19, File 102D, p. 1.

CHAPTER IX
ADMINISTRATIVE ARRANGEMENTS

In many respects, the Antarctic Treaty is an anomaly in international relations. Nowhere is this more apparent than in the way the Consultative Powers have chosen to handle the question of administration. In virtually every other regime or international organization, there is a central bureaucracy or secretariat. The United Nations secretariat in New York and Geneva and the secretariat of the European Community in Brussels are just two such examples. The need for a bureaucracy in most instances is obvious. There must be administrative personnel to handle the day-to-day functioning of the organization or regime. However, the Antarctic Treaty provides for no mechanism.

Although the primary function of any bureaucracy is its administrative responsibility, there is inevitably a secondary function that cannot be ignored. By establishing a secretariat, states create a political lobby within a system, regime or organization dedicated to the preservation of that arrangement. Foreign ministries can change their attitudes towards an agreement, but a bureaucracy that exists because of an agreement possesses a vested interest in preserving the status quo and its own position. Thus, the most die-hard supporters of the UN are the secretariat staff of the UN; the most out-spoken defenders of the European Community are the bureaucrats in Brussels. That no such pressure group exists for the Antarctic Treaty, in part, endangers the agreement of 1959 in that there is no cohesive interest group in favor of preserving the Treaty as a matter of principle. Various lobbies, environmentalist, scientific and political (the Antarctic office of each foreign ministry, but this is hardly a group dedicated to the Treaty itself), take an interest in the Antarctic, but none will defend the present agreement at all costs. The early years of the Treaty addressed the question of "administrative arrangements," and the question was settled within a few years. There would be no secretariat for the Antarctic.

The issue of a secretariat first arose in the interim meetings in Washington in preparation for the First Consultative Meeting in Canberra. During these meetings, the Australian government made it known that it wanted a permanent secretariat headquartered in Canberra and staffed by Australian Foreign Office personnel. As the Australian proposal circulated, Argentina, Chile and the Soviet Union expressed their doubts as to the efficacy of a secretariat. They preferred to continue the Washington interim meetings. Primarily, this preference was due to the fact that all the Consultative Powers were represented there with staff knowledgeable on Antarctic matters; they had been dealing with the issues since 1959, and therefore, were seen as the most experienced and professional personnel to do the job.[1]

In light of this, the Australians modified their position calling instead for its own Foreign Office to perform administrative duties until the next Consultative Meeting; that is, the Australian Foreign Office would manage Antarctic affairs until the Buenos Aires Meeting. The Americans adopted a posture somewhere between the Australians and the South American-Soviet camp. The US supported the idea of continuing the interim meetings while willing to accept Australian administration until the Second Consultative Meeting. A permanent secretariat, though, was unacceptable to the US.[2]

At the First Consultative Meeting, the question of administration filled two days with argument. Australia's desire for a permanent secretariat in Canberra received the support of New Zealand, South Africa and the UK. Against the Commonwealth were the South Americans, fearing the establishment of a "UN for Antarctica," joined by the Soviets, the French and the Belgians.[3]

With so much opposition to Australia's idea, the Meeting tried to evolve interim procedures for consultations; in a sense arranging for a regime without a secretariat. Five rules in furtherance of this compose Recommendation I-XIV: 1) the present host government will send certified conference documents to all parties and supply information, 2) the next host will consult with the others about a date and agenda for the next Meeting, 3) governments will consult on Antarctic quesitons via standard diplomatic channels, 4) all Consultative Powers will be notified of approval of Recommendations by other governments, and 5) the depositary government, i.e., the US government, will carry out rule 4.[4]

At the Second Consultative Meeting, the matter arose again, and much the same debate was carried out as in Canberra. Australia again took the lead in calling for a permanent secretariat. South Africa and the United Kingdom supported the Australians.[5] However, New Zealand defected from the Commonwealth bloc that existed on the issue in 1961 and asked that consultations between Meetings be held in the capital of the next host.[6] This would seem to have been the first proposal for Preparatory Meetings.

Modifying the New Zealand proposal, the US, adamant in its desire to prevent the establishment of a secretariat, urged that the Belgian embassy in Washington be the site of the next round of interim talks. This proposal took into account that the Washington staffs of the various embassies were the most experienced in Antarctic matters and that Belgium had been selected as the next host of a Consultative Meeting. Part of the difficulty in holding interim talks in Belgium was the sparse representation of certain Consultative Powers in Brussels; Argentina had no mission there at all. This situation could cripple preparations. The US was saved from having to speak too vociferously against a secretariat by the French and the Soviets. For their part, the French argued very eloquently against a bureaucracy being established, citing Parkinson's Law, though not by name; that is, they noted that a bureaucracy will tend to make work for itself and that the work will expand to fill the time allowed for its completion.[7] Echoing the French, the Soviet delegate quite sensibly pointed out that the arrangements for interim meetings under Recommendation I-XIV had not been in force for even two months when the Buenos Aires Meeting opened. They argued that the arrangements be given a chance. This view received general support, and no action was taken on the question at the Second Consultative Meeting.[8]

Administrative arrangements did not arise again until the Fourth Preparatory Meeting in Brussels on 5 September 1963. South Africa circulated a paper noting that a number of administrative problems still existed. Essentially, four problems were mentioned: 1) no provisions existed for inter-governmental consultations apart from the Consultative Meetings, despite Treaty provisions and Recommendations, 2) there were no methods of coordinating governmental actions, 3) no way existed to "remind" governments of their obligations under the Treaty and Recommendations, and 4) there were no channels for initiating talks on this.[9] South Africa maintained that because of this very little had really been accomplished on implementing the Canberra proposals, and that too much time had been wasted on the issue in Buenos Aires. Noting that, the South Africans pointed out that the Preparatory Meetings had clearly gone beyond arranging an agenda and were addressing matters of substance, e.g., the Agreed Measures. Bearing in mind the opposition of some nations to establishing a permanent secretariat, South Africa proposed that one person be appointed to handle these problems.[10] Discussion of the proposal was held until the next Preparatory Meeting to allow the delegations time to study and consult on the idea.[11]

On 14 November 1963, the Fifth Preparatory Meeting tackled the South African proposals. However, in the weeks that had passed, the idea had been modified by the South Africans themselves. Their proposal was now cast as a compromise between a permanent secretariat, Washington interim meetings and rotating preparatory meetings. The revised suggestion would create a permanent secretariat with a rotating headquarters; it would move after each Consultative Meeting. It was stressed by the South Africans that this was most timely because the Washington Telecommunications Meeting called for full-time coordination of radio communication. SCAR was reluctantly handling it for the time being, but the secretariat could take the responsibility from SCAR easily.[12]

The US felt this to be premature and that present arrangements were adequate. Argentina agreed, and along with Chile and the Soviet Union, expressed its opposition to the proposal. Support came from Australia and New Zealand, a reversal for the latter since its opposition to a secretariat in Buenos Aries. Britain, however, bolted from the Commonwealth pro-secretariat camp and agreed completely with the US. Belgium, in accepting a secretariat in principle, and favoring its appearance on the agenda, noted that the present system of administration was a compromise based on what was possible in light of the opposition some states expressed towards a secretariat. However, the paper the South Africans had circulated in September promised to overturn the flaws that existed in the system of Preparatory Meetings.[13]

In January of 1964, the Sixth Preparatory Meeting in Brussels convened. When the delegates reached the agenda item on South Africa's proposals for administrative arrangements, the South Africans asked that it not be discussed for the time being. The opposition expressed in November had given them grounds for thought, and they felt that further discussion would only antagonize their opposition.[14]

The South African proposals for administrative arrangements were placed on the agenda at the Ninth Preparatory Meeting over the objections of the Soviets, French, and South Americans. Noting, though, that this point may have delayed the adoption of the agenda, Belgium proposed that each state be prepared to vote on the agenda at the Consultative Meeting point by point.[15] Obviously, a fight over the issue was imminent.

The fight, however, failed to materialize. In the face of strong opposition, the South Africans withdrew their proposal from the agenda of the Third Consultative Meeting. In withdrawing it, South Africa and Britain both maintained that it did not establish a precedent, that "any item may be inscribed on the agenda regardless of objections."[16] This incident, however, is too reminiscent of an earlier argument over a British proposal on criminal jurisdiction for the Buenos Aires Meeting to be ignored. At that time, Chile had objected to discussing the proposal because of its direct legal ties to the matter of territorial sovereignty, and in the second week of the Meeting, the British withdrew the item. Despite reservations to the contrary, a dangerous precedent was established; "if you object loudly enough in Antarctic treaty discussions you can prevent discussion on an item."[17] Although there is little point in forcing a discussion upon one's opponents, the withdrawal of any agenda item in the face of such opposition is probably more damaging in the long-term.

The last discussion of administrative arrangements occurred at the Preparatory Meeting in Santiago in September 1966. Yet again, South Africa proposed discussion of the issue, but having dropped the impossible dream of a permanent secretariat, the South Africans merely suggested discussions centering on more contacts between the Consultative Meetings. The UK, one of the more ardent supporters of some form of administrative arrangements, expressed an interest in stationary consultations, reminiscent of the Washington interim meetings. Argentina, Belgium, Chile, France and the USSR all opposed South Africa's idea. Australia, having made a significant shift in policy over the years, was neutral to the suggestion, glad that there was no secretariat envisoned but not seeing the need for more contacts. The US and New Zealand, preparing for South Africa's withdrawal of the proposals, both maintained that any retraction of the idea would not remove the obligation of the Consultative Powers to consult with one another between the Fourth and Fifth Consultative Meetings. That reservation made, the South Africans withdrew their proposal.[18]

Since the Santiago Preparatory Meeting, there seems to have been no further call for a secretariat for the Antarctic Treaty. Moreover, the separate but related Treaty on Pelagic Sealing does not provide for any centralized bureaucracy; such administration as required is divided between the signatory governments and SCAR. Only the separate

Convention on the Conservation of Antarctic Marine Living Resources has a "Commission," headquartered in Hobart, Tasmania, Australia.[19] Having been signed in 1980, it is too soon to tell if these professional bureaucrats for Antarctica will become an effective pressure group. It is unlikely that they shall because their interest is not in preserving the Treaty but the separate Convention on Living Resources. If their primary political interest were the preservation of the Treaty, they might become a factor by the 1991 review conference, but it is not.

The interesting point about the early years of the Treaty and the proposals for a secretariat for the Treaty is the position each country took. This was not a case of claimants against non-claimants. For Chile and Argentina, the resistance to a secretariat was undoubtedly based on their claim to territorial sovereignty. A secretariat of international character engaged in the administration of the Antarctic certainly undermines any claim to sovereignty. However, the matter of territoriality does not explain Soviet views, let alone those of the pro-secretariat states.

In the case of the Soviet Union, one must remember that the international community of 1961 was much different compared to that of today. Until the creation of many independent, Third World states during the decolonization period of the 1960s and 1970s, the Soviets were outnumbered by western democracies. For example, Stalin insisted that the Ukraine and Byelorussia have representation at the UN, despite their lack of independence, in order to help balance out the preponderance of western members. The Korean War saw the UN fighting for American interests against Soviet ones. Even in the 1960s, the Soviets felt that the world community as it was then composed was hostile to Soviet interests. Given that view of international politics, it is not a surprise, therefore, that the Soviets opposed another international organization in which they would be in the minority and which could be used to further western interests at the expense of the Soviet Union.

The pro-secretariat position of the Commonwealth Consultative Powers has a different basis. Although the Australians, British and New Zealanders have claims to territory in the Antarctic, they supported the idea of an international secretariat. This curious stance can only be understood if one recalls a comment made in the discussions of the Agreed Measures; they proposed a secretariat because of "... their habitual view that Washington should not be allowed to 'take over the Treaty'."[20] If there was a belief in London, Canberra, Wellington and Pretoria that the US was trying to hijack administrative control of the Antarctic Treaty, there could be no better way to foil the attempt than by creating an international secretariat. Indeed, Australia's initial proposal would go further, taking the staff for the bureaucracy from its own Foreign Office and placing the headquarters in Canberra. Although this might appear that the Commonwealth countries were being a bit paranoid, the US did object to a permanent secretariat and was quite content to continue the system of interim meetings, in Washington. Thus, they were prepared to sacri- fice some of their claim to sovereignty in exchange for keeping the administrative control of the system out of American hands.

NOTES

[1]United States, Department of State, "Draft Position Paper on Administrative Arrangements," RG 307, Box 29, File 102.1.1.

[2]*Ibid.*

[3]National Science Foundation, "Trip Report to the First Consultative Meeting," p. 5. South American fears belie the telegram message. "The 64 delegates from the 12 signatory countries are calling this first Meeting on the Antarctic Treaty the Polar United Nations." United States, Department of State, Telegram 915, 830A. From US Embassy Canberra to US Information Agency Washington, 14 July 1961, RG 307, Box 29, File 102.1.1.

[4]Recommendation I-XIV.

[5]National Science Foundation, "Trip Report to the Second Consultative Meeting," p. 4.

[6]United States Navy, "Memo for the Record," p. 4.

[7]National Science Foundation, "Trip Report to the Second Consultative Meeting," p. 4.

[8]United States Navy, "Memo for the Record," p. 4.

[9]South Africa, "Antarctic Treaty Administrative Arrangements," RG 307, Box 17, File 102D.

[10]*Ibid.*

[11]Department of State, Division of Language Services, "Minutes of the Fourth Meeting in Preparation ...", p. 10.

[12]Department of State, "Procès-Verbal de la 5ème Réunion Préparatoire ...", p. 8.

[13]*Ibid.*

[14]Department of State, "Procès-Verbal de la 6ème Réunion Préparatoire ...", p. 7.

[15]Department of State, "Procès-Verbal de la 9ème Réunion Préparatoire ...", pp. 7-8.

[16]Department of State, "Report of the US Delegation to the Third Consultative Meeting," p. 2.

[17]National Science Foundation, "Trip Report to the Second Consultative Meeting," p. 1.

[18]Department of State, "Preparatory Delegation Report," p. 13.

[19]Convention on the Conservation of Antarctic Marine Living Resources, Article XIII.

[20]Department of State, "Report of the US Delegation to the Third Consultative Meeting," p. 6.

CHAPTER X
AN ANTARCTIC MINERALS REGIME?

The present challenge to the continued survival of the Antarctic Treaty System is the entire question of exploiting Antarctica's presumed mineral wealth. If the Consultative Powers can establish a regime governing the extraction of minerals from the Antarctic, the continued functioning of the System seems assured. Failure, on the other hand, would appear to guarantee its collapse on various fronts.

First, the extraction of minerals is by its very nature destructive of the environment. Although it does not invariably damage an ecosystem irreparably, the scale on which extraction would have to be undertaken in Antarctica simply to be economical would ensure some environmental damage. Indiscriminate and unregulated mineral exploitation would inevitably and permanently destroy the Antarctic environment. Apart from the aesthetic loss, Antarctic and sub-Antarctic ecosystems would suffer greatly, reducing or eliminating the region's value to biology and related sciences. Thus, one casualty of failed mineral negotiations is likely to be research science, a vital part of the System.

Second, the right to extract minerals raises questions on taxes to be paid on profits from mineral extraction, regulation and licensing of extractors, and legal jurisdiction over people involved in mineral activities. These, in turn, threaten to open up the issue of territorial sovereignty. Without regulations to address these and other sovereignty matters, the compromise on claims in Article IV of the Treaty will fall apart, and the System is likely to follow suit.

Third, a failure to come to terms on mineral resources will bring internal pressures on the System with it. As of this writing, the possible review of the Treaty is only five years away. A collapse of mineral negotiations is likely to make a review conference more probable, and the discontent engendered by failure on the minerals issue will make amendments to the Treaty more conceivable. As mentioned before, this path can lead to the end of the System quite easily.

Fourth, failure to settle the minerals question will strengthen external opposition to the System. The UN, having resolved the issue of minerals on the seabed with the Law of the Sea Treaty, will be put forward as a rival to the System. If the Consultative Powers have failed with their mineral problem, the UN, already successful with its similar problem, will be pushed by some of its member states toward a more active role in Antarctica. This would almost certainly lead to UN super- vision of the System, if successful. Even if the System survives in some form under UN auspices, the situation will be much different from the present status quo.

All of this, however, presumes that there are minerals in the Antarctic in adequate quantities and qualities to make commercial exploitation possible. Although it is not known that there are or are not, the Consultative Powers are behaving as if there were.

Almost from the beginning of human activity in Antarctica, there has been speculation on the potential mineral resources of the region. On the one hand, Captain James Cook said of the continent that he suspected to lie at the South Pole, "I make bold to declare that the world will derive no benefit from it";[1] two centuries later, when the US Senate was holding hearings on ratification of the Antarctic Treaty, Laurence M. Gould, second-in-command on Admiral Byrd's first expedition, said that he would not give a nickel for the known mineral wealth of the region.[2] On the other hand, traces of chromium, cobalt, nickel and platinum have been found in the Dufek Massif, and copper, lead, gold, silver, tin and zinc exist in low concentration in the Transantarctic Mountains.[3] Also, the US Geological Survey estimates 45 billion barrels of oil and 115 trillion cubic feet of natural gas exists on West Antarctica's continental shelf, although only one-third of that total may be recoverable.[4]

To some, the idea of exploiting Antarctic mineral wealth is unacceptable. Noting the damage to the environment as well as the extreme fragility of the region's ecosystems, their alternative is to declare Antarctica a "World Park". Although there are numerous variations on the scheme, the effect would be to prohibit development of Antarctic mineral deposits. They feel that such development, even when regulated, will pose excessive risks to the environment.

Needless to say, the Consultative Powers have not embraced the World Park concept. At the First Consultative Meeting in Canberra, the British proposed declaring Antarctica a "nature reserve",[5] a suggestion that got nowhere. In more recent times, negotiations on minerals have covered how the exploitation will be regulated rather than if it will be permitted.

There are, however, grounds for optimism for those who oppose such activities. Mineral exploitation is an economic matter, and the economics of the situation may prevent the extraction of minerals from Antarctica. Although it is probable that Antarctica has its share of Earth's minerals, the relative accessibility of Antarctica will inevitable drive up extraction costs. Even when technologically possible, extraction of oil from under the Southern Ocean will be expensive. The mining of platinum, gold, silver, and diamonds from an area covered in a mile-thick ice-sheet clearly will carry high production costs, even if deposits can be located. Antarctica's minerals will only be extracted when it makes business sense to do so; that is, until a profit can be made on it, there will be no mineral extraction in Antarctica. With the falling commodity prices in the 1980s, it is difficult to see when Antarctic mineral activities could be profitable. With the Consultative Powers favoring mineral extraction, the best hope for supporters of the World Park is continued low prices for oil, gold, and other minerals.

Within the System itself, the first hint that the Consultative Powers were acting on the question of Antarctic minerals came at the Sixth Consultative Meeting in Tokyo. Although no Recommendation came of it, the British appear to have raised the issue,[6] perhaps as part of their interest in conservation, but that is not necessarily the case.

Starting at the Seventh Consultative Meeting in Wellington, New Zealand, Recommendations on minerals were issued. For example, Recommendation VII-6 placed minerals on the agenda for the next Consultative Meeting and called for studies on the issue. Recommendation VIII-14, from the Oslo Meeting in June 1975, did the same and in greater detail, including a call for a special Preparatory Meeting on the subject. The report of that Preparatory Meeting was endorsed in Recommendation IX-1 in London in 1977, and a minerals regime was put forward as one possible solution to the question. Recommendation X-1 from the Washington Meeting in 1979, formally proposes such a regime.

For reasons similar to those concerning the convention on pelagic sealing, negotiations on the issue of a minerals regime have been formally separated from the workings of the Treaty itself. Several "Special Consultative Meetings on Antarctic Mineral Resources" have been held in the 1980s. They have been closed to the public, press and non-Treaty states, however, just as the other aspects of the Treaty itself are. Thus, only a hint of the negotiations' progress is available. However, the basis for the discussions, the so-called "Beeby Draft," has been secured.

After discussions with representatives of each Consultative Power, Chris Beeby of New Zealand's Foreign Office prepared an informal working paper based on the views he had heard. The resulting draft treaty, the "Beeby Draft," is just that, a draft possessing no legal impact. However, it does show the collective thinking of the Consultative Powers with regard to a minerals regime.

As a draft, the proposal is, of course, subject to change. The version examined here (and given in full in Appendix B) is a revised draft dated 29 March 1984.[7] Parts may have been deleted, altered and added in the intervening time, but the concepts embodied in the draft are more important than the actual wording of the agreement.

Because it is a draft agreement, its organization is not quite ideal, and a discussion article-by-article would prove confusing rather than illuminating. Therefore, the Beeby Draft will be examined more broadly than were the Treaty and the Agreed Measures.

As envisioned by the Beeby Draft, the Antarctic minerals regime would establish a handful of institutions: a Commission, an Advisory Committee, a Secretariat and Regulatory Committees.[8] The Commission is the supreme body of the regime and is composed of the original signatories of the minerals agreement, acceding states that are Consultative Powers under the Antarctic Treaty, or acceding states that have some request or application pending with the Commission. Acceding states remain Commission members so long as they retain their Consultative Status or until their application has been dealt with.[9] The Advisory Committee has as members all Commission Members and any Party to the regime and the Antarctic Treaty that has done relevant research.[10] The

Secretariat is appointed by the Commission to handle bureaucratic functions and will probably draw its staff from the citizenry of the regime's participants.[11] The membership in each Regulatory Committee will vary and will be discussed later for the sake of clarity.

Any minerals activity in Antarctica is to be undertaken by an "operator." An operator can be a Party to the regime, an agency of a Party (e.g., a national Antarctic minerals company), a natural person, a juridical person (e.g., a private corporation) or a joint venture of any of those. Unless the operator is a Party to the regime, a link of citizenship or corporate control must exist between the operator and a Party, and the Party is that operator's "sponsoring state."[12] Thus, there seems a clear desire to keep non-Parties and their citizens out of Antarctic mineral exploitation.

The first step in the process of exploiting Antarctica's mineral resources is "prospecting." Basically, prospecting is defined as the taking of samples with fairly safe, environmentally speaking, techniques.[13] Any operator may go prospecting without any delay so long as the sponsoring state notifies the Secretariat of various data (e.g., area of prospecting, minerals sought, duration of prospecting, etc.) three months before the prospecting begins.[14] If any Commission members object to the environmental soundness of the techniques or to the location or if prospecting will interfere with other uses of Antarctica, a meeting of the Commission can be convened within three months to review the issue. The Commission can recommend measures to address the problems and the sponsoring state must report back an undecided number of months later on how it implemented those measures.[15]

The second stage in the process is called "exploration." In essence, exploration goes beyond prospecting, allowing drilling, dredging and so on to determine the feasibility of commercial extraction. Exploration, though, does not cover such activities as pilot projects or actual commercial extraction.[16]

Unlike prospecting, exploration can not be undertaken without the permission of the Commission. To secure this permission, a Party to the regime must first secure the Commission's positive determination to allow the submission of applications to explore, and second, it must secure approval of an application.[17]

In the first case, a Party, not necessarily a sponsoring state, must notify the Secretariat that it desires a determination regarding applications, and in the notification, it must supply information on the area to be opened, the mineral resource concerned, the methods of exploration, the environmental impact and so forth.[18] Such a Party is called "the requesting state" and is not the same, necessarily, as a sponsoring state. The Commission reviews the notification after receiving the views of the Advisory Committee and will refuse a notification if an unacceptable environmental risk exists. The Commission is also empowered to alter the boundaries of the area or place conditions upon a positive determination. This is done for each mineral resource, and an area open for applications for gold, for example, would not necessarily be open for those for silver.[19]

Once a positive determination to accept applications has been made, a

Regulatory Committee for the area in question is created. The composition of each Regulatory Committee is determined by an intricate formula, but the practical result is that the requesting state, claimants in whose claim the area lies, the USA and USSR are guaranteed seats on the Regulatory Committee. In addition, the claimants may appoint up to three other Parties providing the total number of claimant states does not exceed four. Then, the Chairman of the Commission appoints non-claimants to the Regulatory Committee so that there is an equal number of claimants and non-claimants, and the total number of members is not to exceed eight.[20] It is the duty of the Regulatory Committees to divide its area of competence into blocks and to establish fees to be paid with the submission of each application for an exploration permit.[21]

After the blocks and fees have been established, sponsoring states may submit their applications. When this is done, the composition of the Regulatory Committee changes. The requesting state (unless it is a superpower or a claimant) is dropped from the Regulatory Committee and is replaced by the sponsoring state. The sponsoring state, in turn, is removed from the Regulatory Committee when a final decision has been made on its application. If this change upsets the claimant to non-claimant ratio, the Chairman appoints new members to restore the balance.[22]

The application itself must contain the same sorts of data as prospecting notifications but with more detail.[23] The Secretariat receives the application and refers it to the competent Regulatory Committee. The Regulatory Committee then makes only two decisions. First, it ascertains that there is a genuine link between the sponsoring state and the operator. Second, it decides whether the operator has the financial resources and the technical expertise to carry out the exploration. If the Regulatory Committee is not satisfied on either of these counts, no further action is taken on the application. If it is satisfied, the application is referred to the Advisory Committee.

It is the duty of the Advisory Committee to determine the degree of environmental risk involved if the application were approved. The advice is sent to the Regulatory Committee. If the Advisory Committee believes too great an environmental risk is involved, the Regulatory Committee can either reject the application or refer it to the Commission. If sent to the Commission, it may be rejected or conditions may be set under which the application could proceed. If the Advisory Committee identifies no great environmental risks, the Regulatory Committee, then, must create a Management Scheme.[24]

In creating a Management Scheme for an area, the Regulatory Committee selects one or more of its members to prepare a draft scheme. The selection is be a simple majority vote, but all claimants in whose claim the area lies as well as the sponsoring state must be part of that majority.[25]

The Management Scheme itself represents the arrangements and rules under which the exploration activities, and development activities later on, will occur. It covers a wide range of issues and concerns from depletion policy and duration of the exploration permit to applicable legal juris-

104

diction and contingency plans in case of accident.[26]

Once drafted, the Management Scheme is presented to the Regulatory Committee for adoption. Once again, approval is by a simple majority vote with the claimants and the sponsoring state possessing a veto. If not approved, the scheme is redrafted. If approved, the scheme then goes to the Commission. The Commission may approve or reject the Management Scheme. If rejected, the Regulatory Committee must redraft the scheme. If the Management Scheme is approved by a 2/3 majority of the Commission's members, a permit for exploration activities is issued in accordance with the provisions of the Management Scheme.[27] The holder of an exploration permit has exclusive rights to explore, and later, develop the mineral resource in that particular block.[28]

The third and final stage in the exploitation of Antarctic minerals as envisioned by the Beeby Draft is "development." Development is specified as following exploration and includes pilot programs, support processing storage and transport activities. In the main, development is the extraction of a mineral resource on a commercial scale.[29] Like exploration, development occurs only after a permit has been granted.[30]

The process for securing a development permit follows that for securing an exploration permit quite closely. While an exploration permit and a Management Scheme are in effect for a specific mineral in a specific block, a sponsoring state may apply for a development permit. The application must provide updated and modified information as required for the exploration permit. The Secretariat, upon receipt of the application, refers it to the Regulatory and Advisory Committees for action.[31]

First, the Advisory Committee reviews the application. Specifically, the Advisory Committee is charged with determining if the application shows any changes in the development activities envisaged when the Management Scheme was adopted and if any unforeseen environmental risks are now apparent. If so, it reports that to the Regulatory Committee along with guidelines for solving those problems.[32]

Next, the Regulatory Committee and Commission must act on the development permit application. It is the responsibility of the Regulatory Committee to modify, when necessary, the Management Scheme in accordance with the guidelines provided by the Advisory Committee. Under no circumstances will this amending process touch on the financial obligations in the Management Scheme. Then, the amended, or original if no ammendments were necessary, Management Scheme goes to the Commission. The Commission *"without further review"* will issue a development permit in accordance with the Management Scheme it received.[33]

It may be unfair to critique the Beeby Draft without knowing the internal debates and divisions that brought about some of its terms. However, the secrecy of the Antarctic Treaty System is chiefly responsible for this condition. Therefore, while it may be unfair to proceed with a critique, those who may suffer an injustice by such criticism are, in part, responsible for it.

To start with the institutions of the regime, it is clear that three critieria have helped shape them. First, universality of membership has been rejected in favor of membership based on participation in the Antarctic Treaty System. Second, the regime appears inherently skewed in favor of exploitation of Antarctica's mineral wealth. Third, the claimant states and the superpowers have been given greater influence in the regime than other Parties.

In the Commission, only the first criterion is apparent. Membership on the Commission is granted in four different ways. Original signatories, acceding Consultative Powers, acceding requesting states and acceding sponsoring states with active applications are Commission members. The parallel here with Consultative status under the Antarctic Treaty is overwhelming. Acceding states are Commission members only so long as they remain Consultative Powers, requesting states or applicant sponsoring states. When their status as such changes, they cease to be members of the Commission. The orginal signatories, though, are permanent members of the Commission. In one respect, the Beeby Draft is superior to the Treaty on the matter of membership, and that is its provisions for observer status. Any Party to the regime and any Commission-approved international organization may act as observers. Under the Treaty, there was no such provision and only recently did the Contracting Parties win observer status at Consultative Meetings. A further step for the Beeby Draft would be opening Commission meetings to the public. Although it is typical of Antarctic politics that no such provision exists, it is difficult to imagine any decision or debate the Commission would have to undertake *in camera*.

In the Advisory Committee, this same view prevails. All Commission members are members of the Advisory Committee; therefore, the later inherits the problems of the former. Also, membership is open to any Party to the Antarctic Treaty that has done relevant research into Antarctic minerals. This might seem to mean Consultative Powers but not necessarily. Because some Consultative Powers can lose their Consultative status, this measure allows them to retain input into the technical body, although they lose membership in the Commission (unless they were an original regime member). Once again, the Treaty System is preferred over universality of membership. Observer status here is somewhat broader than in the Commission extending to not just Parties to the regime but also to the Treaty members and Commission-approved international organizations, including non-governmental ones. Once again, public meetings would improve this, but the explicit reference to non-governmental bodies is important. The environmentalist lobby might be more supportive of the regime if their views were formally taken into consideration. Because they are not states, and therefore lack the status of subjects of international law, there are fundamental problems in granting them anything more than observer status. It is, though, a positive step. The Beeby Draft would be further strengthened if an explicit reference to non-governmental organizations appeared in Article X concerning the Commission's membership, but their inclusion in the Advisory Committee as observers is important.

In the Regulatory Committees, where the nuts and bolts of mineral exploitation are to be handled, all three criteria arise. Membership in the Regulatory Committees is restricted to Commission members, not just Parties to the regime, the most exclusive membership of any of the regime's institutions. Moreover, there is no provision at all for observers. Although observers' input into decisions of the Commission and Advisory Committee will help keep the regime "honest," direct input from observers at the Regulatory Committee level would do even more. One suspects, however, that this omission was intentional and probably the result of an entrenched negotiating position on the part of one or more states.

With regard to skewing the regime toward pro-exploitation states, one must first acknowledge that it is unlikely that a state opposed to it would join the regime. However, there are varying degrees of interest. Some states will likely oppose all but the safest exploitation while others will take a more lenient attitude. Even so, the regime favors the more lenient. This is best shown by a look at the membership of the Regulatory Committees.

First of all, the claimant states are likely to favor exploitation of minerals under most circumstances. This is particularly true if they can secure, in the Management Scheme or elsewhere, royalties, taxes and/or licensing fees. As claimants, they may be able to assert some right to the proceeds from exploitation, and rarely do governments refuse revenues.

Next, there is the requesting state or applicant sponsoring state. Common sense dictates that no request or application would exist if the state were not marginally interested in exploitation. They, too, may be entitled to taxes or other revenues from the activity.

Third, and somewhat more problematical in this analysis, are the superpowers. Despite their differences, they are united in their traditions of exploiting mineral deposits where, when and how they choose. Given their past record of mineral exploitation elsewhere it is reasonably safe to assume that the Soviets and Americans will favor exploitation of minerals when feasible economically. Ecological concerns will be secondary.

Finally, there are the members appointed by the claimants. If it is logical to assume that the claimants will favor exploitation of minerals, it is equally logical to assume that the members of the Regulatory Committee that they appoint will support their view. Although the Chairman of the Commission may appoint virulent opponents to mineral extraction, the numerical balance will favor exploitation.

As an example, if a Regulatory Committee were to be established for an area which was in territory claimed by a single state, one may presume the membership to have at least four pro-exploitation members straight away: the claimant, the requesting or sponsoring state, the USA and the USSR. Depending on whether the requesting or sponsoring state is a claimant, either two or three members may be appointed by the claimant in whose claim the area lies. As mentioned, these are almost certain to favor extraction, bringing the total to six or seven members who favor the principle of mineral exploitation. In balancing the number of claimants and non-claimants, the Chairman of the Commission can do little to balance pro- and anti-exploitation members. The US and USSR are non-claimants who are likely to favor extraction and are members of each Regulatory Committee. Thus, the Chairman may appoint nor more than two anti-exploitation members. Votes of six to two could be expected, if two anti-exploitation members can be found among the Commission's members.

On the third criteria, it is obvious that the claimants and the super-powers are given much more influence that non-claimant states. Clearly, this is an attempt to remove the question of territorial sovereignty from the regime without actually addressing the issue overtly. This interpreta-tion is given credence by the wording of the clause that gives the US and USSR a place on every Regulatory Committee. They are not referred to by name but as "the two states which, prior to entry into force of the Antarctic Treaty, had asserted a basis of claim in Antarctica."[34] Their place in the Regulatory Committees is, thus, tied to territorial sovereignty. Since their potential claims are not demarcated, they are given representa-tion on each Regualtory Committee, and this allows any claimant or potential claimant a voice in regulating an area that it may claim. Naturally, this may only be camoflage for the superpowers' insistence on greater influence than other states possess. In any case, claimants and the superpowers, for whatever reason, are given more influence than other Parties to the regime.

In other ways, the Beeby Draft suffers from poor timing in the review of activities. For example, three months' notice is required before pros-pecting may begin and during that time, the Commission may consider the proposal. As a hypothetical case, if notice were received exactly three months before prospecting were to begin and if it took two months for a member of the Commission to notice a problem, only one month would remain for a meeting to be arranged. Moreover, if the Commission were not convened for the three months allowed by the agreement, two months' prospecting, potentially damaging in nature, could have occur-red. Although it is hoped that some sort of moratorium would be insti-tuted, this conflicts with the right of operators to prospect without any permission being granted. To solve this problem, at least six months notice should be required before prospecting begins. Ideally, this sort of difficulty will be ironed out as negotiations progress, but it is not certain that it will.

More generally, the environmental protections are often qualified by phrases like "in so far as it is feasible" or "to the extent possible" and risks tend to warrant action only if they are "significant." These qualifiers will only lead to disputes. "Feasible," for example, may mean one thing to an environmentalist and quite another to a mining company. "Significant risk" is a similar term. Almost any human activity in Antarctica presents an environmental risk of some kind, yet many risks could be defended as being "insignificant." In a way, this criticism is seeking legal certainty in the inexact and uncertain world of diplomacy, but the regime must be as iron-clad as possible if it is to function.

This is not to condemn the Beeby Draft or the ideas it embodies. There are some terms and provisions in it that benefit not just the regime's Parties but any other group with an interest in the Antarctic.

In breaking the extraction process into three distinct phases, prospecting, exploration and development, the Beeby Draft does create a machinery to monitor the progress of the activities. Greater environmental protection would exist if prospecting required a permit and if the Commission could reject a Management Scheme during consideration of a development permit application. Despite that, the arrangements established are sound. It may be wished that the Advisory Committee had power to do more than just advise, but its position within the regime is almost identical to the position of Meetings of Experts under the Treaty. Whether for good or ill, the precedent set by the workings of the Treaty is being followed by the Beeby Draft.

In addition, parts of the Beeby Draft make provisions for accommodating other international bodies and their concerns. For example, the Commission is instructed to cooperate with the UN, SCAR and the International Union for the Conservation of Nature.[35] More importantly, the regime specifically excludes the deep seabed from its area of application,[36] and it requires the Commission to cooperate with "any international organization which may have competence in respect of mineral resources in areas adjacent to those covered by this regime."[37] The only conceivable mineral deposits adjacent to Antarctica's are on the seabed. Thus, the Beeby Draft consciously acknowledges the Seabed Authority's interest and jurisdiction over seabed mineral deposits, *de facto* if not *de jure*. This should confer a greater degree of legitimacy on the Antarctic minerals regime than if an accommodation with the Law of the Sea agreement were ignored.

On balance, the Beeby Draft tries to allow for some protection of the Antarctic environment but does so only to a degree and at the price of the creation of a bureaucracy. It clearly supports the Antarctic Treaty System, but its purpose is to alter the nature of human activity in the region, commerce instead of science.

Turning to the actual events relating to the mineral negotiations, one encounters a vacuum of data. Like all other Antarctic negotiations, the governments involved are doing their utmost to keep them secret. However, there have been facts collected and released to the public. Although by no means do they allow for even an imprecise account to be written, they are relevant to the subject at hand and give a sense of the atmosphere in which the negotiations are being conducted.

On matters of environmental protection, it appears that the British have kept their policy constant in trying to safeguard Antarctica's environment. Although they seemed to desire an amendment to the Agreed Measures to allow "incidental mortality" of fauna,[38] the British proposed stringent environmental impact assessment procedures along with monitoring of key indicators and consideration of cumulative impacts of mineral activities at the Twelfth Consultative Meeting in Canberra in September 1983.[39] This would appear to be part of the guiding principles in the Beeby Draft, Article III(d) (iii). Despite Soviet opposition, the British proposals were referred to SCAR for Consideration.[40] When SCAR had completed its study, the Soviets appear to have kept the Consultative Powers from considering a Recommendation supporting it.[41]

Another point of interest is the form the minerals regime is to take. Once again, some debate seems to have existed over whether a separate treaty seems the preferred choice,[42] but this demonstrates the consistency of Antarctic politics. The same discussion occurred in Brussels in the mid-1960's on conservation.

On political matters, there has been a significant development, the increased participation of Contracting Parties to the Treaty. These states were first allowed observer status at the Consultative Meeting in 1983, the Twelfth in Canberra. However, they were denied the same position for the Special Consultative Meetings on Antarctic Mineral Resources.[43] At an "Informal Consultation on Minerals" in Tokyo in 1984, the Netherlands requested observer status. Although Chile, India and Brazil supported the request, the Dutch were kept out by opposition from the Soviets and others. Although Chris Beeby briefed the Dutch and others afterwards, the briefing was said to be "lacking in substance".[44] Thus, as the Special Consultative Meeting in Paris in 1985, the Contracting Parties held their own caucus, and Beeby provided them with some of the conference documents.[45] This growing activism of the Contracting Parties is a significant development because it opens the System to all states. An instrument of accession is all that is required to participate. While the gap between Consultative and Contracting status persists, the Contracting Parties are pressing for a voice of some kind.

Finally, three other points should be mentioned. First, Beeby suggested in Autumn 1985 expanding the number of Regulatory Committee members to ten and setting aside one non-claimant seat for develop- ing states.[46] Second and related to that, Chile proposed establishing a fund to aid developing states in Antarctic research.[47] Third, Norway has adopted a position of "full liability" in Antarctic mineral resource activities;[48] an operator would have unlimited liability done to the Antarctic environment. While it is far too early to tell what will become of these suggestions, they do point the direction various facets of the negotiations have taken.

The creation of a regime is inherently a difficult diplomatic issue, and one for Antarctic minerals is no exception. However, the Consultative Powers seem to be moving towards a successful conclusion based on some version of the Beeby Draft. Only time will tell if their efforts will bear fruit, though.

NOTES

[1]Philip Quigg, *A Pole Apart*, p. 3.

[2]United States, Senate, "Antarctic Treaty" Hearings, Committee on Foreign Relations, 86th Congress, 2nd Session, 1960.

[3]Philip Quigg, *A Pole Apart*, p. 88.

[4]Jonathan Spivak, "Frozen Assets", *Wall Street Journal*, 21 February 1974, *passim*.

[5]United States, Department of State, "Draft Position Paper on Conservation of Antarctic Living Resources", RG 307, Box 29, File 102.1.1.

[6]United States, Senate, "US Antarctic Policy" Hearings, Subcommittee on Oceans and International Environment, Committee on Foreign Relations, 94th Congress, 1st Session, 1975. Testimony of Dixy Lee Ray.

[7]For the earlier version, see *ECO* (Vol. XXIII, No. 1, July 1983), and for a critique of the first version, see Jeff Myhre, "What Not to Do about Antarctic Mineral Rights", *Wall Street Journal (Europe)*, 21 July 1983, p. 10.

[8]See Chapter II of the Beeby Draft.

[9]Article X(2).

[10]Article XVI(2).

[11]Article XXI.

[12]Article V.

[13]See Article II(1)(j).

[14]Article XXIII.

[15]Article XXIV(bis).

[16]Article II(1)(g).

[17]See Chapter IV of Beeby Draft.

[18]Article XXV(2).

[19]Article XXVI.

[20]Article XX.

[21]Article XXVI(bis).

[22]Article XX(4) and (5).

[23]Article XXVII(d).

[24]Article XXVIII.

[25]Article XXIX.

[26]Article XXX.

[27]Article XXXI.

[28]Article XXXII(1).

[29]Article II(h).

[30]See Chapter V of the Beeby Draft.

[31]Article XXXIV.

[32]Article XXXV(1), (2), and (3).

[33]Article XXXV(4), (5), (6). Emphasis added.

[34]Article XX(3)(c).

[35]Article XXXVI(2).

[36]Article VI(1).

[37]Article XXXVI(3).

[38]*ECO.* (Vol. XXXIV, No. 1, 7-18 October 1985), pp. 1 and 4.

[39]*ECO.* (Vol. XXVI, No. 1, 18-27 January 1984), p. 1.

[40]*ECO.* (Vol. XXVI, No. 2, 18-27 January 1984), p. 3.

[41]*ECO.* (Vol. XXXIV, No. 2, 7-18 October 1985), p. 1.

[42]*ECO.* (Vol. XXVI, No. 1, 18-27 January 1984), p. 7.

[43]*Ibid.*, p. 1.

[44]*ECO.* (Vol. XXVII, No. 2, 22-31 May 1984), p. 3.

[45]*ECO.* (Vol. XXXIII, No. 2, 23 September-4 October 1985), p. 3.

[46]*Ibid.*, No. 1, pp. 1-2.

[47]*Ibid.*, p. 2.

[48]*Ibid.*, No. 2, p. 2.

CHAPTER XI
THE FUTURE OF THE
ANTARCTIC TREATY SYSTEM

Thus far, the main issues challenging the survival of the Antarctic Treaty System have arisen out of the System itself. The politics of Antarctica have centered on making the System function and on addressing disputes arising out of human activities in the region. However, there is another dimension that cannot be ignored as the possibility of a review conference in 1991 grows closer; that is, the composition of the international community in which the System exists has changed drastically since the Treaty was signed in 1959.

During the 1950s when the foundations of the System were being laid, the community of nations was beginning to expand as the result of decolonization. However, the western developed states still possessed overwhelming influence. The newly-independent states were preoccupied with the creation of political and economic institutions and with the process of nation-building. Although India tried to put the question of Antarctica on the agenda of the UN General Assembly in 1956 and 1958 (and withdrew the item both times),[1] the largely western members of the Antarctic Treaty were left to act unopposed.

In the 1960s and 1970s, decolonization accelerated, and the developing states of the Third World began demanding changes in the structure of intenational society. Examples of this growing discontent with the status quo include the establishment of the Non-Aligned Movement and calls for a New International Economic Order and a New International Information Order.

With this shift in the composition of the world community and the increased interest on the part of the new states in a wide range of issues, it is hardly surprising that the 1980s have seen Third World demands for a change in the way Antarctica is administered. For example, at the Seventh Conference of the Heads of State or Government of the Non-Aligned Movement in New Delhi in March 1983, the final declaration took note of Antarctica's significance, including its economic importance, to the world.[2] Then in July 1985, the Council of Ministers of the Organization of Africa Unity (OAU) passed a resolution declaring Antarctica to be a common heritage of mankind.[3]

Although these sorts of resolutions, statements and declarations are useful indicators of official thinking in the Third World, they will not, on their own, alter the international environment in which the Treaty System must function. Their attack on the System is not on the grounds that it is a failure or ineffective but rather on the grounds that its membership is too restrictive to be just. Consequently, only a body of universal membership is an appropriate rival for the status quo. To their credit, the Non-Aligned Movement and the OAU have recognized this in their statements on Antarctica. They attack the legitimacy of the System on the basis of its limited membership and argue that the UN, as the only universal political body in the international community, should oversee the Antarctic.

This particular dispute, between those who argue for universal participation in decisions and between those who argue that only those actively involved in a matter should be involved in the decision-making, is not unique to the Antarctic. The same argument arose in the question of the Seabed Authority and can even be seen in the disputes in South Africa and the Middle East. However, it does represent a different sort of problem for the Antarctic System.

Setting aside the abortive attempts by India to involve the UN in the Antarctic in the 1950s, the first action the UN took with regard to the region occurred in 1983. In a letter to the Secretary-General dated 11 August 1983, Malaysia and Antigua and Barbuda requested that the "Question of Antarctica" be placed on the agenda of the UN's 38th session. On 23 September, the matter was referred to the First Committee, which considered the issue 28-30 November. The First Committee's report recommended the passage of a resolution sponsored by an exclusively Third World group: Antigua and Barbuda, Bangladesh, Malaysia, Pakistan, the Philippines, Singapore, Sri Lanka and Thailand.[4] This recommendation was accepted by the General Assembly, passing it on 15 December 1983. The resolution instructed the Secretary-General to prepare a study on Antarctica.[5]

In the Secretary-General's report, there is little that is new to a student of Antarctica. It addresses the geophysical position of the continent, the rival claims of sovereignty and the Antarctic Treaty itself.[6] Most of it, though, is given over to statements by several countries on their policy toward Antarctica.[7] Although useful, there is little here that comes as a surprise either. For example, Nigeria and Pakistan oppose the present System without reservation.[8] Uruguay, which had just acceded to the Treaty and which would shortly receive Consultative status, supported the System strongly.[9]

In the 39th session of the UN in 1984, Antarctica remained on the agenda. Although the resolution passed that session only thanked the Secretary-General for his report and put the matter on the agenda for the next session, the resolution did make one significant point. It recalled the Non-Aligned Movement's 1983 declaration,[10] and thereby implied a certain sympathy with that group's position.

Of far greater importance was the resolution passed the following year during the 40th session of the UN in 1985. Divided into three parts, it is the most comprehensive statement that the UN has made on Antarctica to date. Section A calls for the Secretary-General to update and expand the 1984 study and puts the question on the agenda for the 41st session. Section B addresses the minerals regime negotiations, specifically calling for "equitable sharing of benefits" of mineral exploitation, and for the Consultative Powers to inform the Secretary-General of the state of their negotiations. Section C notes the participation of South Africa in the System and its apartheid policies, requesting that the other Consultative Powers exclude South Africa from Consultative Meetings.[11]

Clearly, the UN is beginning to consider seriously the Antarctic situation. Speculation on where that will lead is difficult because the UN's interest is so new. Despite that, there are some points about it that can be made. While accurate forecasting cannot be done, certain factors influencing Antarctica's future with regard to the UN are already apparent.

First among these is the entire question of whether the UN can enforce its will to any degree in the Antarctic. Because the resolutions of the General Assembly are not binding, these annual parliamentary exercises are likely to serve only as a gauge of world opinion on Antarctica. The only way to put teeth into these moves would be to pass them in the Security Council, which can pass binding resolutions. The difficulty here is that the veto exists in the Security Council and those states that possess it are Consultative Powers. They have little incentive to permit the Security Council to act against the Antarctic System.

The next point, which may work to the benefit of the System's opponents, is the timing of the UN's interest. As provided for in Article XII paragraph 2 of the Antarctic Treaty, a review conference may be held 30 years after the Treaty enters into force, that is, in 1991. Presuming the conference is convened in 1991, any amendments passed by a majority of Contracting Parties, which must include a majority of Consultative Powers, must be ratified by 1993, and if they are not, states may begin withdrawing from the Treaty in 1995. It is obvious that the increasing interest of the UN in the years immediately before the review conference is likely to put pressure on the System for major alterations in the System. Whether this pressure will influence the System hinges on two factors: first, a review conference may not be held and second, the changes in membership in the System itself may undercut the UN's claim to greater legitimacy than the System has.

For a review conference to be held in 1991 or after, a Consultative Power must request that it be held.[12] Presuming a successful settlement of the minerals issue, it is difficult to see what motivation a Consultative Power would have to request a review conference. The sole purpose of such a conference is to amend the Treaty, and by way of the Consultative Meetings, a Consultative Power already has a forum for amending the Treaty. The difference is that a Consultative Meeting can amend the Treaty only by unanimous consent, whereas a majority of Contracting States, including a majority of Consultative Powers, can amend the agreement at a review conference. In either case, amendment of the Treaty can result in withdrawals from the agreement. Thus, a Consultative Power must believe an amendment is vital enough to risk withdrawals, and the problems arising from that and must believe that the majority of Contracting States is easier to secure than the unanimous agreement of Consultative Powers. Only the matter of a minerals regime appears to be vital enough to warrant the risks and controversial enough to make unanimity difficult. Failure of the minerals negotiations might yield a review conference; success on minerals makes a review conference of questionable value.

The other development that may prevent the UN's interest in Antarctica from having any effect on the situation is the expansion of membership in the Antarctic System. From the original 12 signatories, the number of states in the System has grown to 32, and 18 of these are Consultative Powers. Third World participation has increased with the addition of Brazil, India, the People's Republic of China and Uruguay to the Consultative list. With countries such as Spain, which has acceded to the Treaty and overtly aspires to Consultative status,[13] there are several more potential Consultative Powers waiting in the wings. This growth makes the System much less exclusive and, therefore, more able to resist UN attacks on its legitimacy. With all the permanent members of the Security Council also holding Consultative status and with such important members of the Third World as Brazil and India holding the same status, it is less likely that the UN can make effective use of its growing interest in Antarctica.

There is, of course, always the possibility that these new participants in Antarctic politics have joined the System with the intent of sabotaging it, but that appears to be an excessively cynical reading of their policies. More likely, they believe that they are better able to bring about reforms of the System from within than by staying outside it. Thus, while the System will be influenced by the input from these new members, the external pressure from the UN will not be as effective as it would otherwise be. Whatever change occurs will be evolutionary and from within as opposed to revolutionary from outside the System.

The entire question of South African participation in the System raised another sort of difficulty. With its racial policies, South Africa is the target of much UN hostility, and undoubtedly the 1985 General Assembly resolution is only the first of many calls for excluding South Africa from the System. As an original signatory of the Treaty, though, South Africa cannot legally be removed without its own consent.[14] A diplomatic stalemate is almost inevitable, with many countries demanding South Africa's exclusion and with South Africa's insisting on its rights. Since the roots of the problem do not lie in Antarctica but in southern Africa, the resolution of this problem can only come with a solution to the racial issue in southern Africa. However, it will not greatly effect the Antarctic Treaty System.

In the past, South African participation in the System has been a minor irritant. For example, unofficial but accurate reports reached the delegates to the Santiago Preparatory Meeting on 6 September 1966 that the South African Prime Minister had been assassinated. The delegates drew up a declaration of sympathy which was read the following day. The Soviets, however, as harsh critics of South Africa, arrived diplomatically late and missed the reading of the statement.[15] The Santiago Meeting was otherwise unaffected by South African participation. It is reasonable to assume that, with more anti-apartheid states joining the System, more noise will be made about South Africa's presence at meetings of whatever sort, but there is little reason to believe it will be any more effective in Antarctic politics that it has been elsewhere.

In light of all this, the Antarctic Treaty System seems to be on a sound footing and capable of surviving more or less unchanged into the twenty-first century. If a solution to the question of mineral exploitation can be found, the System should certainly continue, and the 1991 review conference may not be summoned. The UN's interest in Antarctica may have helped prompt the expansion in the number of Contracting Parties and Consultative Powers in the 1980s, but ironically, this very growth should, in the end, create greater legitimacy for the System. In turn, this strengthens the System against UN intervention in Antarctic politics.

NOTES

[1]United Nations, Secretary-General, "Question of Antarctica", A/39/583, Vol. I, part 1, p. 21.

[2]Greenpeace International, "Future of Antarctica", Appendix VIII, p. 1.

[3]*Ibid.*, pp. 1-2.

[4]United Nations, First Committee, "Question of Antarctica", A/38/646, p. 2.

[5]United Nations, General Assembly, "Question of Antarctica", A/Res/38/77.

[6]Secretary-General, "Question of Antarctica", Vol I, part 1.

[7]*Ibid.*, Vol I, part 2 and Vols. II and III.

[8]*Ibid.*, Vol. I, part 2, pp. 21-2 and 32-36.

[9]*Ibid.*, Vol. III, p. 133.

[10]United Nations, First Committee, "Question of Antarctica", A/C.1/39/L.83.

[11]United Nations, General Assembly, "Question of Antarctica", A/Res/40/156.

[12]Article XII, paragraph 2 of the Antarctic Treaty.

[13]Secretary-General, "Question of Antarctica", Vol. III, p. 70.

[14]See Chapter III on Antarctic Treaty Article IX.

[15]United States, Department of State, "General Comments on the Draft Fourth Consultative Meeting Preparatory Report", RG 307, Box 18, File 102D, pp. 1-2.

APPENDIX A:
THE ANTARCTIC TREATY

The governments of Argentina, Australia, Belgium, Chile, the French Republic, Japan, New Zealand, Norway, the Union of Soviet Socialist Republics, the United Kingdom of Great Britain and Northern Ireland, and the United States of America,

Recognizing that it is in the interest of all mankind that Antarctica shall continue forever to be used exclusively for peaceful purposes and shall not become the scene or object of international discord;

Acknowledging the substantial contributions to scientific knowledge resulting from international cooperation in scientific investigation in Antarctica;

Convinced that the establishment of a firm foundation for the continuation and development of such cooperation on the basis of freedom of scientific investigation in Antarctica as applied during the International Geophysical Year accords with the interests of science and the progress of all mankind;

Convinced also that a treaty ensuring the use of Antarctica for peaceful purposes only and the continuance of international harmony in Antarctica will further the purposes and principles embodied in the Charter of the United Nations;

Have agreed as follows:

ARTICLE I

1. Antarctica shall be used for peaceful purposes only. There shall be prohibited, *inter alia*, any measures of a military nature, such as the establishment of military bases and fortifications, the carrying out of military maneuvers, as well as the testing of any type of weapons.
2. The present Treaty shall not prevent the use of military personnel or equipment for scientific research or for any other peaceful purpose.

ARTICLE II

Freedom of scientific investigation in Antarctica and cooperation toward that end, as applied during the International Geophysical Year, shall continue, subject to the provisions of the present Treaty.

ARTICLE III

1. In order to promote international cooperation in scientific investigation in Antarctica, as provided for in Article II of the present Treaty,

the Contracting Parties agree that, to the greatest extent feasible and practicable:

(a) information regarding plans for scientific programs in Antarctica shall be exchanged to permit maximum economy and efficiency of operations;

(b) scientific personnel shall be exchanged in Antarctica between expeditions and stations;

(c) scientific observations and results from Antarctica shall be exchanged and made freely available.

2. In implementing this Article, every encouragement shall be given to the establishment of cooperative working relations with those Specialized Agencies of the United Nations and other international organizations having a scientific or technical interest in Antarctica.

ARTICLE IV

1. Nothing contained in the present Treaty shall be interpreted as:

(a) a renunciation by any Contracting Party of previously asserted rights of or existing claims to territorial sovereignty in Antarctica;

(b) a renunciation or diminution by any Contracting Party of any basis of claim to territorial sovereignty in Antarctica which it may have whether as a result of its activities or those of its nationals in Antarctica, or otherwise;

(c) Prejudicing the position of any Contracting Party as regards its recognition or non-recognition of any other State's right of or claim or basis of claim to territorial sovereignty in Antarctica.

2. No acts or activities taking place while the present Treaty is in force shall constitute a basis for asserting, supporting or denying a claim to territorial sovereignty in Antarctica or create any rights of sovereignty in Antarctica. No new claim, or enlargement of an existing claim, to territorial sovereignty in Antarctica shall be asserted while the present Treaty is in force.

ARTICLE V

1. Any nuclear explosions in Antarctica and the disposal there of radioactive waste material shall be prohibited.

2. In the event of the conclusion of international agreements concerning the use of nuclear energy, including nuclear explosions and the disposal of radioactive waste material, to which all of the Contracting Parties whose representatives are entitled to participate in the meet- ings provided for under Article IX are parties, the rules established under such agreements shall apply in Antarctica.

ARTICLE VI

The provisions of the present Treaty shall apply to the area south of 60° South Latitude, including all ice shelves, but nothing in the present Treaty shall prejudice or in any way affect the rights, or the exercise of the rights, of any State under international law with regard to the high seas within that area.

ARTICLE VII

1. In order to promote the objectives and ensure the observance of the provisions of the present Treaty, each Contracting Party whose representatives are entitled to participate in the meetings referred to in Article IX of the Treaty shall have the right to designate observers to carry out any inspection provided for by the present Article. Observers shall be nationals of the Contracting Parties which designate them. The names of observers shall be communicated to every other Contracting Party having the right to designate observers, and like notice shall be given of the termination of their appointment.
2. Each observer designated in accordance with the provisions of paragraph 1 of this Article shall have complete freedom of access at any time to any or all areas of Antarctica.
3. All areas of Antarctica, including all stations, installations and equipment within those areas, and all ships and aircraft at points of discharging or embarking cargoes or personnel in Antarctica, shall be open at all times to inspection by any observers designated in accordance with paragraph 1 of this Article.
4. Aerial observation may be carried out at any time over any or all areas of Antarctica by any of the Contracting Parties having the right to designate observers.
5. Each Contracting Party shall, at the time when the present Treaty enters into force for it, inform the other Contracting Parties, and thereafter shall give them notice in advance, of
   (a) all expeditions to and within Antarctica, on the part of its ships or nationals, and all expeditions to Antarctica organized in or proceeding from its territory;
   (b) all stations in Antarctica occupied by its nationals and
   (c) any military personnel or equipment intended to be introduced by it into Antarctica subject to the conditions prescribed in paragraph 2 of Article I of the Treaty.

ARTICLE VIII

1. In order to facilitate the exercise of their functions under the present Treaty, and without prejudice to the respective positions of the Contracting Parties relating to jurisdiction over all other persons in Antarctica, observers designated under paragraph 1 of Article VII and scientific personnel exchanged under sub-paragraph 1(b) of Article III of the Treaty, and members of the staffs accompanying such persons, shall be subject only to the jurisdiction of the Contracting Party of which they are nationals in respect of all acts or omissions occurring

while they are in Antarctica for the purpose of exercising their functions.

2. Without prejudice to the provisions of paragraph 1 of this Article, and pending the adoption of measures in pursuance of sub-paragraph 1(e) of Article XI, the Contracting Parties concerned in any case of dispute with regard to the exercise of jurisdiction in Antarctica shall immediately consult together with a view to reaching a mutually acceptable solution.

ARTICLE IX

1. Representatives of the Contracting Parties named in the preamble to the present Treaty shall meet at the City of Canberra within two months after the date of entry into force of the Treaty, and thereafter at suitable intervals and places, for the purpose of exchanging information, consulting together on matters of common interest pertaining to Antarctica, and formulating and considering, and recommending to their Governments, measures in furtherance of the principles and objectives of the Treaty, including measures regarding:
   (a) use of Antarctica for peaceful purposes only;
   (b) facilitation of scientific research in Antarctica;
   (c) facilitation of international scientific cooperation in Antarctica;
   (d) facilitation of the exercise of the rights of inspection provided for in Article VII of the Treaty;
   (e) questions relating to the exercise of jurisdiction in Antarctica;
   (f) preservation and conservation of living resources in Antarctica.
2. Each Contracting Party which has become a party to the present Treaty by accession under Article XIII shall be entitled to appoint representatives to participate in the meetings referred to in paragraph 1 of the present Article, during such time as that Contracting Party demonstrates its interest in Antarctica by conducting substantial scientific activity there, such as the establishment of a scientific station or the dispatch of a scientific expedition.
3. Reports from the observers referred to in Article VII of the Treaty shall be transmitted to the representatives of the Contracting Parties participating in the meetings referred to in paragraph 1 of the present Article.
4. The measures referred to in paragraph 1 of this Article shall become effective when approved by all Contracting Parties whose representatives were entitled to participate in the meetings held to consider those measures.
5. Any or all of the rights established in the present Treaty may be exercised as from the date of entry into force of the Treaty whether or not any measures facilitating the exercise of such rights have been proposed, considered or approved as provided in this Article.

ARTICLE X

Each of the Contracting Parties undertakes to exert appropriate efforts, consistent with the Charter of the United Nations, to the end that no one engages in any activity in Antarctica contrary to the principles or purposes of the present Treaty.

ARTICLE XI

1. If any dispute arises between two or more of the Contracting Parties concerning the interpretation or application of the present Treaty, those Contracting Parties shall consult among themselves with a view to having the dispute resolved by negotiation, inquiry, mediation, conciliation, arbitration, judicial settlement or other peaceful means of their own choice.

2. Any dispute of this character not so resolved shall, with the consent, in each case, of all parties to the dispute, be referred to the International Court of Justice for settlement; but failure to reach agreement on reference to the International Court shall not absolve parties to the dispute from the responsibility of continuing to seek to resolve it by any of the various peaceful means referred to in paragraph 1 of this Article.

ARTICLE XII

1. (a) The present Treaty may be modified or amended at any time by unanimous agreement of the Contracting Parties whose representatives are entitled to participate in the meetings provided for under Article IX. Any such modification or amendment shall enter into force when the depositary government has received notice from all such Contracting Parties that they have ratified it.

   (b) Such modification or amendment shall thereafter enter into force as to any other Contracting Party when notice of ratification by it has been received by the depositary Government. Any such Contracting Party from which no notice of ratification is received within a period of two years from the date of entry into force of the modification or amendment in accordance with the provisions of sub-paragraph 1(a) of this Article shall be deemed to have withdrawn from the present Treaty on the date of the expiration of such period.

2. (a) If after the expiration of thirty years from the date of entry into force of the present Treaty, any of the Contracting Parties whose representatives are entitled to participate in the meetings provided for under Article IX so requests by a communication addressed to the depositary Government, a Conference of all the Contracting Parties shall be held as soon as practicable to review the Treaty.

   (b) Any modification or amendment to the present Treaty which is approved at such a Conference by a majority of the Contracting Parties there represented, including a majority of those whose representatives are entitled to participate in the meetings provided for under Article IX, shall be communicated by the depositary

Government to all Contracting Parties immediately after the termination of the Conference and shall enter into force in accordance with the provision of paragraph 1 of the present Article.

(c) If any such modification or amendment has not entered into force in accordance with the provisions of sub-paragraph 1(a) of this Article within a period of two years after the date of its communication to all the Contracting Parties, any Contracting Party may at any time after the expiration of that period give notice to the depositary Government of its withdrawal from the present Treaty; and such withdrawal shall take effect two years after the receipt of the notice by the depositary Government.

ARTICLE XIII

1. The present Treaty shall be subject to ratification by the signatory States. It shall be open for accession by any State which is a member of the United Nations, or by any other State which may be invited to accede to the Treaty with the consent of all the Contracting Parties whose respresentatives are entitled to participate in the meetings provided for under Article IX of the Treaty.

2. Ratification of or accession to the present Treaty shall be effected by each State in accordance with its constitutional processes.

3. Instruments of ratification and instruments of accession shall be deposited with the Government of the United States of America, hereby designated as the depositary Government.

4. The depositary Government shall inform all signatory and acceding States of the date of each deposit of an instrument of ratification or accession, and the date of entry into force of the Treaty and of any modification or amendment thereto.

5. Upon the deposit of instruments of ratification by all signatory States, the present Treaty shall enter into force for those States and for States which have deposited instruments of accession. Thereafter the Treaty shall enter into force for any acceding State upon the deposit of its instrument of accession.

6. The present Treaty shall be registered by the depositary Government pursuant to Article 102 of the Charter of the United Nations.

ARTICLE XIV

The present Treaty, done in the English, French, Russian and Spanish languages, shall be deposited in the archives of the Government of the United States of America, which shall transmit duly certified copies thereof to the Governments of the signatory and acceding states.

APPENDIX B:
THE BEEBY DRAFT AGREEMENT ON AN
ANTARCTIC MINERAL RESOURCE REGIME

(as of 29 March 1984)

The Parties to the regime,

(a) *Recalling* the provisions of the Antarctic Treaty;

(b) *Convinced* that the Antarctic Treaty system has proved effective in promoting international harmony in furtherance of the purposes and principles of the United Nations Charter, in ensuring the protection of the Antarctic environment and in promoting freedom of scientific research in Antarctica;

(c) *Reaffirming* that it is in the interests of all mankind that the Antarctic Treaty Area shall continue forever to be used exclusively for peaceful purposes and shall not become the scene or object of international discord;

(d) *Noting* that increasing interest in the possibility that exploitable mineral resources may exist in Antarctica;

(e) *Recognizing* that Antarctic mineral resource activities, should they occur, could adversely affect the unique environment of Antarctica and of its dependent or associated ecosystems;

(f) *Aware* of the responsibility of the Antarctic Treaty Consultative Parties to ensure that any activities in Antarctica, including mineral resource activities, should they occur, are consistent with all the principles and purposes of the Antarctic Treaty system;

(g) *Noting* the unique ecological and scientific value of Antarctica and the importance of Antarctica to the world environment;

(h) *Believing* that the protection of the Antarctic environment and of its dependent or associated ecosystems must be a basic consideration in decisions taken on possible Antarctic mineral resource activities;

(i) *Concerned* to ensure that Antarctic mineral resource activities should not disrupt scientific investigation in Antarctica or other legitimate uses of Antarctica;

(j) *Believing* that the adoption of a regime for Antarctic mineral resources will further strengthen the Antarctic Treaty system;

(k) *Convinced* that participation in Antarctic mineral resource activities should be open to all states, and their nationals, which have an interest in such activities and subscribe to a regime governing them;

(l) *Believing* that the effective regulation of Antarctic mineral resource activities is in the interests of all mankind; *have agreed* as follows:

CHAPTER 1: (General)

<u>Article I</u> (Definitions)

1. For the purposes of this regime:
   (a) "Antarctic Treaty" means the Antarctic Treaty done at Washington on 1 December 1959;
   (b) "Antarctic Treaty area" means the area to which the provisions of the Antarctic Treaty apply in accordance with Article VI of that Treaty;
   (c) "Antarctic Treaty Consultative Parties" means the Contracting Parties to the Antarctic Treaty whose representatives are entitled to participate in meetings provided for under Article IX of that Treaty;
   (d) "Antarctic mineral resource activities" means activities relating to prospecting or exploration for, or development of, mineral resources in the area to which this regime applies, but does not include scientific research activities within the meaning of Article III of the Antarctic Treaty;
   (e) "Convention on the Conservation of Antarctic Marine Living Resources" means the Convention drawn up at Canberra on 20 May 1980;
   (f) "Convention on the Conservation of Antarctic Seals" means the Convention done at London on 19 June 1972;
   (g) "Exploration" means activities aimed at identifying and evaluating specific mineral resource occurrences or deposits, including exploratory drilling, dredging and other surface or subsurface excavations required to determine the nature and size of mineral resource deposits and the feasibility of their development but excluding pilot projects or commercial production;
   (h) "Development" means those activities which take place following exploration which are aimed at or associated with exploitation of specific mineral resource deposits, including but not limited to, pilot projects and support processing storage and transport activities;
   (i) "Operator" means any participant in Antarctic mineral resource activities meeting the requirements of Article V of this regime;
   (j) "Prospecting" means activities aimed at identifying areas of mineral resource potential, including but not limited to, geological, geochemical and geophysical means and field observations, the use of remote sensing techniques and collecting of surface and seafloor samples but does not include dredging or other surface or subsurface excavations, except for the purpose of obtaining samples, or drilling other than shallow drilling which is both known to be off geological structures and does not exceed a depth of [ ] meters;
   (k) "mineral resources" means all non-living natural non-renewable resources, including but not limited to, fossil fuels, metallic and non-metallic minerals;
   (l) "Sponsoring State" means the Party to this regime designated as

such in accordance with Article V and includes any Party to this regime conducting Antarctic mineral resource activities on its own behalf.

Article II (Objectives and Principles)

1. The objective of this regime is to provide a means, through the institutions it creates, the principles it establishes and the rules it prescribes, for:
   (a) assessing the possible impact on the Antarctic environment of Antarctic mineral resource activities;
   (b) determining whether Antarctic mineral resource activities are acceptable;
   (c) governing the conduct of such Antarctic mineral resource activities as may be found acceptable;
   (d) ensuring that any Antarctic mineral resource activities are undertaken in strict conformity with the provisions of this regime, including the principles established by it.
   2. All Antarctic mineral resource activities shall be conducted in accordance with the following general principles:
   (a) decisions about Antarctic mineral resource activities shall be based upon information adequate to enable informed judgments to be made about their possible impact;
   (b) Antarctic mineral resource activities shall be conducted in an orderly, safe, efficient and rational manner;
   (c) Antarctic mineral resource activities shall be conducted on the basis of the environmental principles set out in Article III, in such a manner as to avoid damage to the Antarctic environment and its dependent or associated ecosystems, upsetting the ecological balance of Antarctica or damaging or destroying any area, object or installation of historical value or scientific interest;
   (d) the Antarctic Treaty Consultative Parties shall retain an active and responsible role in relation to all proposed or actual Antarctic mineral resource activities;
   (e) the conduct of research necessary to make informed environmental and resource management decisions shall be promoted;
   (f) scientific investigation and other legitimate uses of Antarctica shall be protected to the fullest extent possible;
   (g) the interests of all mankind in Antarctica shall not be prejudiced;

Article III (Environmental Principles)

The following environmental principles shall be applicable to Antarctic mineral resource activities undertaken by operators and to the making of decisions within the institutions created by this regime:
(a) no Antarctic mineral resource activities shall take place until an impact assessment has been completed and a reasonable judgement,

based on adequate information has been made that the activities in question will not:

(i) cause significant degradation of Antarctic atmospheric, terrestrial, and marine environments and their associated ecosystems from which effective recovery is not probable within a reasonable period of time;

(ii) prejudice the implementation of Article II of the Convention for the Conservation of Antarctic Marine Living Resources;

(iii) have any but minimal local effects;

(iv) affect global or regional climate or weather patterns;

(v) disturb atmospheric, terrestrial, and marine environments and their dependent or associated ecosystems beyond the area of this regime.

(b) such judgements shall not be made unless there is adequate information available to:

(i) predict, within reasonable margins of error, the normal operating impact of the activities in question;

(ii) identify the nature of possible accidents and assess the risks of such accidents occuring;

(iii) predict the impact of such accidents should they occur;

(c) the information on which such judgements are based should also include appropriate baseline studies of the areas most likely to be affected by the activities in question;

(d) in making such judgements, account shall be taken of:

(i) the need to preserve the capacity to monitor, in Antarctica, global environmental parameters;

(ii) the aesthetic value of Antarctica as a part of the earth relatively undisturbed by man;

(iii) the possibility that the cumulative impact of Antarctic mineral resource activities and other activities, each environmentally acceptable in itself, may give rise to the need to avoid additional environmental stress;

(e) no Antarctic mineral resource activities shall take place until technology is available and procedures (including contingency plans in the event of accidents) are established to ensure compliance with the principles stated in paragraph (a) of the Article and to reduce to a reasonable minimum the normal operating impacts, the risk of accidents and the possible impact of accidents should they occur;

(f) no Antarctic mineral resource activities shall take place unless adequate provision is made for:

(i) monitoring key environmental and ecosystem components;

(ii) adapting operating procedures in the light of the results from monitoring, increased knowledge of the Antarctic environment and ecosystems, and the availability of improved technology;

(iii) the removal of structures and installations no longer required and the restoration of the Antarctic environment, to the extent feasible, during the conduct of the activities in question and following their completion.

Article III (bis) (No Activities outside Regime)

No Antarctic mineral resource activities shall be conducted except in accordance with this regime and measures adopted pursuant to it and, in the case of exploration and development, with the specific terms and conditions of a Management Scheme adopted pursuant to Article XXXI or Article XXXV.

Article IV (Area of Application)

1. This regime shall apply to all mineral resource activities taking place on the continent of Antarctica and all other land areas south of 60° south latitude, including all ice shelves, and the seabed and sub-soil of their corresponding [continental shelves] [offshore areas] [continental shelves or offshore areas] but without encroachment on the deep seabed.
2. To the extent necessary the Parties to this regime shall establish, by agreement, the precise northern limits of the area defined in paragraph 1 of this Article.

Article V (Participation in Antarctic mineral resource activities)

1. Antarctic mineral resource activities may be conducted, subject to the provisions of this regime, by:
   (a) a Party to this regime;
   (b) an agency or instrumentality of a Party to this regime;
   (c) a natural person;
   (d) a juridical person;
   (e) a joint venture consisting of any of the foregoing hereinafter referred to as an "operator".
2. Each operator, other than a Party, shall have a substantial and genuine link with a Party (hereinafter referred to as the "sponsoring state"). In the case of a natural person he or she shall have the nationality of a Party. In the case of a juridical person, it shall have its central management and control and substantial resources located in the territory of a Party and be established under the laws of such Party.
3. In the case of a joint venture consisting of any combination of a Party, an agency or instrumentality of a Party, a natural person or a juridical person, the Party to the regime in which the central management and control and substantial resources of the joint venture are located shall be the sponsoring state.
4. In the case of a joint venture consisting of two or more Parties, the participating states shall, by agreement, determine which state shall be the sponsoring state for the purpose of this regime.

Article VI (Compliance)

1. Each Party to this regime shall take appropriate measures within its

competence to ensure compliance with the regime and any measures adopted pursuant to it.

2. Each Party to the regime shall notify the Secretariat established pursuant to Article XXI, for the circulation to all other Parties, of the measures taken pursuant to paragraph 1 of this Article.

3. The Commission established by Article X shall draw the attention of all Parties to the regime to any activity, which in the opinion of the Commission, affects the implementattion of the objectives or principles of this regime or the compliance of any Party with its obligations under this regime.

Article VI (bis) (Responsibility/Liability)
[no formal draft exists]

Article VII (Provision to ensure that Article IV of the Antarctic Treaty is not affected)

Nothing in this regime and no acts or activities taking place while this regime is in force shall:

(a) constitute a basis for asserting, supporting or denying a claim to territorial sovereignty in the Antarctic Treaty area or create any rights of sovereignty in the Antarctic Treaty area;

(b) be interpreted as a renunciation or diminution by any Party of, or as prejudicing, any right or claim or basis of claim to territorial sovereignty in Antarctica or to exercise coastal state jurisdiction under international law within the area to which this regime applies;

(c) be interpreted as prejudicing the position of any Party as regards its recognition or non-recognition of any such right, claim or basis of claim;

(d) affect the provision of Article IV, paragraph 2 of the Antarctic Treaty that no new claim, or enlargement of an existing claim, to territorial sovereignty in Antarctica shall be asserted while the Antarctic Treaty is in force.

Article VIII (links with the Antarctic Treaty and the Antarctic Treaty System)

1. Parties to the regime, whether or not they are Parties to the Antarctic Treaty, agree that they will not engage in any activities in the Antarctic Treaty area contrary to the principles and purposes of that treaty and that in their relations with each other they are bound by the principles and objectives contained in Articles I,II, III, IV, V, VI, VII, and VIII of that Treaty.

2. Parties to the regime, whether or not they are Parties to the Antarctic Treaty, acknowledge the special obligations and responsibilities of the Antarctic Treaty Consultative Parties for the protection and preservation of the environment of the Antarctic Treaty area.

3. Parties to the regime, whether or not they are Parties to the Antarctic

Treaty, shall, with respect to their activities within the area to which this regime applies, observe:

(a) the Agreed Measures for the Conservation of Antarctic Fauna and Flora and such other measures as have been recommended by the Antarctic Treaty Consultative Parties in fulfillment of their responsibility for the protection of the Antarctic environment from all forms of harmful human interference;

(b) any area set aside for special protection under the Convention for the Conservation of Antarctic Marine Living Resources;

(c) any area set aside for special protection under the Convention for the Conservation of Antarctic Seals;

(d) any area which, for historic, ecological, environmental, scientific or other reasons, the Commission has designated as a prohibited area. Such areas, as appropriate, shall be brought to the attention of the Antarctic Treaty Consultative Parties for possible designation as Specially Protected Areas or Sites of Special Scientific Interest.

Article IX (Non-Discrimination)

In the application of the provisions of this regime there shall be no discrimination on the grounds of nationality.

Article IX (bis) (Other uses of Antarctica)

1. Antarctic mineral resource activities shall be conducted so as to respect and protect, to the fullest extent possible, other uses of Antarctica which are consistent with the Antarctic Treaty, including:

(a) stations and associated installations, including support facilities and equipment in Antarctica;

(b) programs of scientific investigation in Antarctica and cooperation toward that end;

(c) the conservation and rational use of Antarctic marine living resources;

(d) tourism conducted in accordance with guidelines approved by the Antarctic Treaty Consultative Parties;

(e) historic monuments protected in accordance with measures adopted by the Antarctic Treaty Consultative Parties;

(f) navigation.

Article IX (ter) (Confidentiality of Data)

1. Subject to paragraph 6 of Article XXIII, operators shall not be required to exchange or make freely available data obtained from Antarctic mineral resource activities.

2. In adopting rules pursuant to paragraph 1 (g) of Article XIII the Commission established by Article X shall ensure that the confidentiality of proprietary data is protected.

132

Article IX (quater) (Notifications)

Where, in any provision of this regime, there is a reference to the provision of information, a notificatiion or a report to any institution provided for in this regime and that institution has not been established, the notification or report shall be provided to the Depositary which shall circulate the information, notification or report as required.

CHAPTER II: (Institutions)

Article X (Commission)

1. The Parties to the regime agree to establish and maintain the Antarctic Minerals Resources Commission (hereinafter referred to as the "Commission".
2. Membership of the Commission shall be as follows:
   (a) each Party to the regime which participated in the meeting at which the regime was adopted shall be a member of the Commission;
   (b) each Party to the regime which has acceded to it pursuant to Article [ ] shall be a member of the Commission during such time as it is an Antarctic Treaty Consultative Party;
   (c) each Party to the regime which has acceded to it pursuant to Article [ ] and which has requested the Commission to make a determination pursuant to Article XXV, shall be a member of the Commission during such time as the Commission is considering any aspect of that request;
   (d) each Party to the regime which has acceded to it pursuant to Article [ ] and which has lodged an application for an exploration permit pursuant to Article XXVII shall be a member of the Commission during such time as the Commission is considering any aspect of that application, including any resulting management scheme or any modification to it.
3. Each member of the Commission shall be represented by one representative who may be accompanied by alternate representatives and advisers.
4. Observer status in the Commission shall be open to:
   (a) any Party to the regime;
   (b) such relevant international organizations as may be specified by the Commission.

Article XI (Convening of the Commission)

1. The first meeting of the Commsion, held for the purposes of taking organizational, financial and other decisions necessary for the effective functioning of the regime and its institutions, shall be convened within [ ] months of the entry into force of the regime.
2. Thereafter and until such time as the Commission decides it to be necessary to establish a regular schedule of meetings, whether

annually or otherwise, meetings of the Commission shall be held within three months of:

(a) the lodging of a request, supported by [ ] members of the regime for a review of prospecting in accordance with paragraphs 2 and 3 of Article XXIV (bis);

(b) a notification requesting the Commission to make a determination pursuant to Article XXV authorizing the submission of applications for exploration and development in respect of an identified area;

(c) a request by not less that [ ] members of the Commission.

3. Until otherwise decided by the Commission, the Depositary shall be responsible for convening its meetings.

Article XII (Commission Procedure)

1. The Commission shall elect from among its members a Chairman and Vice-Chairman, each of whom shall serve for a [ ] period. The Chairman and Vice-Chairman shall not be representatives of the same Party.

2. The Commission shall adopt and amend as necessary rules of procedure for the conduct of its meetings. Such rules may include provisions concerning the number of terms of office which a Chairman or Vice-Chairman may serve and for the rotation of such offices.

3. The Commission may establish, by consensus, such subsidiary bodies as are necessary for the performance of its functions.

4. The official languages of the Commission shall be English, French, Russian and Spanish.

5. The Commission may decide to establish a permanent headquarters at a site to be determined.

6. The Commission shall have legal personality and shall enjoy in the territory of each of the Parties such legal capacity as may be necessary to perform its functions and achieve the objectives of this regime.

7. The privileges and immunities to be enjoyed by the Commission, the Secretariat and representatives attending meetings in the territory of a Party shall be determined by agreement between the Commission and the Party concerned.

Article XIII (Functions of the Commission)

1. The function of the Commission in fulfilment of the objective set out in Article II and in accordance with the principles set out in that Article and in Article III, shall be:

(a) to determine in accordance with Article XXVI whether or not to authorize the submission of applications for exploration and development in respect of an identified area;

(b) to facilitate and promote the collection and exchange of scientific, technical and other information and research projects necessary to assess the possible environmental impaact of Antarctic mineral

134

resource activities;

(c) to designate those areas where for historic, ecological, environmental or scientific reasons Antarctic mineral resource activities should be prohibited;

(d) to formulate, adopt and revise measures relating to the protection of the Antarctic environment and the promotion of safe and effective exploration and development techniques;

(e) to adopt measures relating to prospecting in accordance with Article XXIV and XXIV (ter);

(f) to review prospecting in accordance with Article XXIV (bis);

(g) to adopt rules to elaborate, and ensure the effective operation of, the provisions of Article XIII(3) and (4), Article XXV(2), Article XXVII(2) and Article XXXIV(2) which require the submission to the institutions of the regime of information, notification and reports;

(h) to adopt the budget for the institutions of the regime:

(i) to adopt rules regarding fees to be submitted together with notifications submitted pursuant ot Article XXV and applications submitted pursuant ot Articles XXVII and XXXIV:

(j) to adopt rules regarding levies payable by operators;

(k) to adopt, by consensus, appropriate measures, in order to avoid monopoly situations;

(l) to elaborate by consensus the principle set forth in Article IX with a view to ensuring full and fair opportunity, without discrimination, for participation in Antarctic mineral resource activities;

(m) to establish rules with respect to maximum block sizes;

(n) to authorize the issue of exploration and development permits in accordance with paragraph 2 of Article XXXI and paragraph 6 of Article XXXV;

(o) to consider monitoring reports received pursuant to Article XXXIII;

(p) to establish measures to ensure participation by the international community in possible benefits derived from the regime;

(q) to keep under review the operation of Antarctic mineral resource activities with a view to safeguarding the protection of the Antarctic environment in the interests of all mankind;

(r) to carry out such other functions as are specified elsewhere in the regime or are necessary to fulfill the objective and principles of the regime;

2. In exercising its functions under paragraph 1 the Commission shall take full account of the recommendations and advice of the Advisory Committee, established under Article XVI.

3. The Commission shall ensure that a publicly available record of its decisions and of reports submitted to it is maintained.

Article XIV (Activities by non-Parties)

1. Parties to the regime undertake to exert appropriate efforts, consistent

with the Charter of the United Nations, to the end that no one engages in any Antarctic mineral resource activities contrary to the objective or principles of this regime.

2. The Commission shall draw the attention of any state which is not a Party to this regime to any activity undertaken by its nationals or vessels which, in the opinion of the Commission, affects the implementation of the objective or principles of this regime.

Article XV (Decision-making in the Commission)

1. Except as provided elsewhere in this regime, decisions of the Commission on matters of substance shall be taken by a majority of two-thirds of the members present and voting. The question of whether a matter is one of substance shall be treated as a matter of substance.

2. Decisions on matters other than those referred to in paragraph 1 of this Article or provided for elsewhere in this regime shall be taken by a simple majority of the members present and voting.

Article XVI (Scientific, Technical and Environmental Advisory Committee)

1. Parties to the regime agree to establish and maintain the Scientific, Technical and Environmental Advisory Committee (hereinafter referred to as "The Advisory Committee").

2. Membership of the Advisory Committee shall be as follows:
   (a) Parties to the regime which are members of the Commission;
   (b) any Party to the regime which is a Party to the Antarctic Treaty and which has conducted scientific research relevant to Antarctic mineral resource activities.

3. Observer status in the Advisory Committee shall be open to any Party to the regime, and Party to the Antarctic Treaty and such relevant international organizations, including non-governmental organizations, as may be specified by the Commission.

4. Each member of the Advisory Committee shall be represented by one representative with suitable qualifications who may be accompanied by alternate representatives and by other experts and advisers.

5. The Advisory Committee shall elect from amongst its members a Chairman and Vice-Chairman each of whom shall serve for a [ ] period. The Chairman and Vice-Chairman shall not be representatives of the same Party.

6. The Advisory Committee may seek the advice of other scientists and experts as may be required on an ad hoc basis.

7. The Advisory Committee shall;
   (a) give public notice of matters which it has under consideration and
   (b) receive views on such matters from international organizations having a scientific, technical or environmental interest in them.

8. The Advisory Committee shall adopt and amend as necessary its rules of procedure. Such rules may include provision concerning the

number of terms of office which a Chairman or Vice-Chariman may serve and for the rotation of such offices.

9. The Advisory Committee may, with the approval of the Commission, establish such subcommittees as may be necessary for the performance of its functions.

10. The official languages of the Advisory Committee shall be English, French, Russian and Spanish.

Article XVII (Convening of the Advisory Committee)

1. Unless the Commission decides otherwise, the Advisory Committee shall be convened for its first meeting within [ ] months of the first meeting of the Commission. It shall meet thereafter as often as it may be necessary to enable it to fulfill its functions on the basis of a schedule established by the Commission.

2. Special meetings of the Advisory Committee, in addition to those scheduled pursuant to paragraph 1 of this Article, may be convened at the request of [ ] of the members of the Advisory Committee.

3. Until otherwise decided by the Commission meetings of the Advisory Committee shall be convened by the Depositary.

Article XVIII (Functions of the Advisory Committee)

1. The functions of the Advisory Committee shall be to advise the Commission and the Regulatory Committees. To this end it shall:
   (a) provide a forum for consultation and cooperation concerning the collection, exchange and evaluation of ecological, technical and other information bearing on Antarctic mineral resource activities;
   (b) identify the types of ecological, technical and other information which would be required in order to carry out its functions;
   (c) consider and make recommendations on research projects which would assist in assessing the possible environmental impact of Antarctic mineral resource activities;
   (d) make recommendations concerning areas where Antarctic mineral resource activities should be prohibited;
   (e) provide advice to the Commission in accordance with paragraph 4 of Article XXV relating to a notification requesting the Commission to make a determination authorizing the submission of applications for exploration and development in respect of an identified area;
   (f) provide advice to the Commission in accordance with Article XXVI concerning the modification of the boundaries of an area identified;
   (g) make recommendations, in elaboration of the principles of Article III, as to measures relating to the protection of the Antarctic environment and the promotion of safe and effective exploration and development techniques, including equipment specifications, sea-

sonal or area operating requirements, monitoring, safety or other technical conditions;

(h) provide advice to the Regulatory Committee in accordance with paragraphs 5 and 6 of Article XXVIII in connection with applications for exploration permits;

(i) identify and make recommendations to the Commission in connection with the elaboration of Article XXIII(3) and (4), Article XXV(2), Article XXVII(2) and Article XXIV(2) which require the submission to the institutions of the regime of information, notification and reports;

(j) monitor exploration and development activities in accordance with Article XXXIII;

(k) carry out such other functions as are specified elsewhere in this regime or as may be directed by the Commission.

2. Reports of the Advisory Committee shall be issued regularly and shall reflect the views expressed by all members of the Committee. Such reports shall be circulated to all Parties to the regime and shall also be published.

Article XIX (Decision-making by Advisory Committee)

1. Except as provided elsewhere in this regime, decisions of the Advisory Committee on matters of substance shall be taken by a majority of two-thirds of the members present and voting. The question of whether a matter is one of substance shall be treated as a matter of substance.

2. Decisions on matters other than those referred to in paragraph 1 of this Article or provided for elsewhere in this regime shall be taken by a simple majority of the members present and voting.

Article XX (Regulatory Committee)

1. For each identified area in respect of which the Commission has made a determination pursuant to Article XXVI authorizing the submission of applications for exploration and development, there shall be a separate Regulatory Committee.

2. Subject to the provisions of paragraph 5 of this Article, the Regulatory Committee shall consist of not more than eight states.

3. Each Regulatory Committee shall consist of:
   (a) the Party or Parties (if any) which assert a right of or claims to sovereignty in the identified area;
   (b) the Party which submitted the notification pursuant to Article XXV in respect of the identified area (hereinafter referred to as "the requesting state");
   (c) the two states which, prior to the entry into force of the Antarctic Treaty had asserted a basis of claim in Antarctica;
   (d) up to three Parties which are members of the Commission designated by the Party or Parties referred to in (a) above, provided that the total number of Parties appointed to the Regulatory Commit-

tee pursuant to (a), (b), (c) and (d) which assert rights of or claims in Antarctica shall not exceed four;

(e) additional Parties which are members of the Commission, selected by the Chairman of the Commission, in consultation with the Chairman of the Advisory Committee, so as to ensure that the Committee consists of an equal number of members which assert rights of or claims to sovereignty in Antarctica and of members which do not assert such rights or claims and so as to include, so far as possible, any Parties which contributed substantial scientific, technical or environmental information to the determination made by the Commission under Article XXVI.

4. At such time as the Regulatory Committeee has referred to it an application made by a sponsoring state under Article XXVII, the following arrangements shall apply:

(a) the requesting state, unless it is also the sponsoring state or is also a member of the Regulatory Committee by virtue of a provision of paragraph 3 of this Article other than paragraph 3(b), shall cease to be a member of the Regulatory Comittee.

(b) the sponsoring state which lodged the application under Article XXVII, if it is not already a member by virtue of the application of the provisions of paragraph 3 of this Article, shall become a member for so long as the Committee is considering any aspect of the application it has made, including any resulting management scheme, or any modification of it.

5. In the event that the application of the provisions of paragraph 4 of this Article results in a disturbance of the balance in membership of the Committee as between members which assert rights of or claims to sovereignty in Antarctica, and members which do not assert such rights or claims the Chairman of the Commission shall select such further Parties which are members of the Commission as may be necessary to ensure that the balance is maintained. In making that selection the Chairman shall accord priority to members of the Commission which have not previously or have least recently served on a Regulatory Committee.

6. Any Party selected pursuant to paragraph 5 of this Article shall serve on the Regulatory Committee only so long as the sponsoring state appointed pursuant to paragraph 4(b) of this Article participates as a member.

7. The designation referred to in paragraph 3(d) of this Article shall be made within 30 days of a determination made by the Commission, pursuant to Article XXVI, to authorize the submission of applications for exploration and development in respect to the identified area.

Article XX (bis) (Regulatory Committee Procedure)

1. The first meeting of each Regulatory Commitee constituted in accordance with Article XX shall be convened by the Depositary in accordance with paragraph 1 of Article XXVI (bis). Each Regulatory Com-

mittee shall meet thereafter when and where necessary to fulfill its functions.

2. Each member of the Regulatory Committee shall be represented by one representative who may be accompanied by alternate representatives and advisers.
3. Each Regulatory Committee may elect from among its members a Chairman and Vice-Chairman. The Chairman and Vice-Chairman shall not be representatives of the same Party.
4. Any Party to the regime may attend meetings of the Regulatory Committee as an observer.
5. Each Regulatory Committee shall adopt and amend as necessary it rules of procedure for the conduct of its meetings.

Article XX (ter) (Functions of Regulatory Committee)

1. The functions of each Regulatory Committee shall be:
   (a) to identify specific blocks within its area of competence and establish fees to be submitted with any application of exploration and development in respect of such blocks in accordance with Article XXVI (bis);
   (b) Terms and Conditions/Guidelines/Indicative Guidelines: Article XXVI [bis(3)];
   (c) to consider applications for exploration permits in accordance with Article XXVIII;
   (d) to designate one or more of its members in accordance with Article XXIX to prepare a draft management scheme;
   (e) to adopt management schemes in accordance with Article XXXI;
   (f) to monitor exploration and development activities in accordance with Article XXXIII;
   (g) to review and undertake any necessary revision in a management scheme in accordance with its terms or at the development stage in accordance with Article XXXV;
   (h) Such other functions as may be specified elsewhere in this regime.

Article XX (quater) (Decision-making in Regulatory Committees)

1. Except as provided in paragraph 3 of Article XXIX and paragraph 1 of Article XXI, decisions of each Regulatory Committee shall be taken by a simple majority of members present and voting.

Article XXI (Secretariat)

1. The Commission may establish a Secretariat to serve the Commission, the Advisory Committee and Regulatory Committes and any subsidary bodies established.
2. The Commission may appoint an Executive Secretary, who shall be the head of the Secretariat, according to such procedures and on such terms and conditions as the Commission may determine. His term of

office shall be for four years and he shall be eligible for re-appointment.

3. The Commission may, with due regard to the need for efficiency and economy, authorize such staff establishment for the Secretariat as may be necessary and the Executive Secretary shall appoint, direct and supervise such staff according to such rules and procedures and on such terms and conditions as the Commission may determine.

4. The Secretariat shall perform the functions specified in this regime and entrusted to it by the Commission, the Advisory Committee and the Regulatory Committees.

Article XXII (Financial Provisions)

1. The Commission shall make budgetary provision for its activities, the activities of the Advisory Committee, Regulatory Committees, any subsidiary bodies established and the Secretariat.

2. The budget shall be financed by:
   (a) fees prescribed pursuant to Articles XIII(1) (i) and XXXVI(bis)(2)(b);
   (b) levies on operators in accordance with rules adopted by the Commission pursuant to Article XIII(1)(j); and
   (c) until such time as the budget is fully financed by fees and levies in accordance with (a) and (b) above, equal contributions from each member of the Commission.

3. Decisions on budgetary matters shall be taken by consensus.

4. The financial activities of the Commission, the Advisory Committee, Regulatory Commitees, any subsidiary bodies established and the Secretariat, shall be conducted in accordance with financial regulations adopted by the Commission and shall be subject to an annual audit by external auditors selected by the Commission.

5. Each member of the Commission, the Advisory Committee, Regulatory Committee and any subsidary bodies established shall meet its own expenses arising from attendance at meetings.

6. A member of the Commission that fails to pay its contribution for two consecutive years shall not, during the period of its default, have the right to participate in any of the institutions of the regime.

CHAPTER III: (Prospecting)

Article XXIII (Prospecting)

1. Any operator may, without further authorization, undertake prospecting within the area to which this regime applies.

2. The sponsoring state shall notify the Secretariat in the event that it or an operator under its sponsorship wishes to engage in prospecting.

3. Such notification shall be made at least three months in advance of the commencement of the planned prospecting activity. It shall:
   (a) identify, by reference to coordinate of latitude and longitude or specific geographical features, the area in which the prospecting is

to occur;

(b) provide information concerning the resources which are to be the subject of the prospecting;

(c) specify the prospecting methods to be used including, in the case of prospecting involving drilling or dredging or excavating for the purpose of taking samples, details concerning those methods;

(d) provide information on any support facilities proposed;

(e) provide an assessment of the environmental impact of the prospecting activity and describe the measures to be adopted to avoid harmful environmental consequences;

(f) in the case of prospecting to be undertaken by an operator other than a Party, certify:

   (i) that the operator has the necessary financial resources and technical expertise to conduct the prospecting in compliance with the provisions of the regime and any measures adopted pursuant to it, and;

   (ii) that the operator has the substantial and genuine link with the sponsoring state required by Article V and provide details of such link;

(g) specify the anticipated duration of the prospecting activity;

(h) such other information as may be required in rules established by the Commission.

4. The sponsoring state shall provide to the Secretariat:

(a) notification of any changes in the information provided pursuant to paragraph 2 and 3 of this Article;

(b) a notification of the cessation of the prospecting activity;

(c) a general report, submitted annually during such time as the prospecting is taking place, on that activity.

5. Notifications and reports submitted pursuant to this Article shall be circulated to all Parties to the regime without delay.

6. No longer than [ ] years after the cessation of the prospecting activity the observations and results obtained from it shall be exchanged and made freely available by the sponsoring state, provided that:

(a) if the observations and results relate directly to an area in respect of which any Party has made a request of the Commission to make a determination pursuant to Article XXV, the period shall be extended for a further [ ] years;

(b) if the observations and results relate directly to a block in respect of which the sponsoring state has lodged an application for an exploration permit pursuant to Article XXVII and that application has not been declined, this paragraph shall not apply.

Article XXIV (Limitations on Prospecting)

1. Prospecting shall no confer any rights or title to resources upon the prospector.

2. Prospecting shall at all times be conducted in compliance with the provisions of this regime, including the principles set out in Article II and Article III, and with measures adopted pursuant to this regime.

3. In the case where more than one operator is engaged in prospecting in the same general area and in the case where both prospecting and exploration or development are being undertaken in an area identified pursuant to Article XXVI, the operators exercizing their right to undertake prospecting shall do so with due regard to the rights of others.

4. Where prospecting is undertaken by an operator other than a Party, the sponsoring state shall take appropriate measures to ensure that the requirements of paragraphs 2 and 3 of this Article are met.

5. Should it consider it necessary to do so, the Commission may adopt additional measures relating to prospecting. Such measures, which shall be consistent with the provisions of this Article and of Article XXIII may:

   (a) classify prospecting activities according to the impact they are likely to have on the Antarctic environment and prescribe additional requirements (which may include the lodging of bonds) for those activities such as drilling or dredging or excavating for the purpose of taking samples or the establishment of permanent or semi-permanent installations, which may present a larger hazard to that environment;

   (b) establish rules to regulate potential conflicts between prospecting and other legitimate uses of Antarctica protected by this regime;

   (c) elaborate, in relation to situations where there may be a concentration of prospecting activities in one general area, the obligation imposed by paragraph 3 of this Article.

Article XXIV (bis) (Review of Prospecting)

1. Any Party to this regime may, on reciept of a notification submitted pursuant to Article XXIII or at any subsequent time, request the sponsoring state to provide further particulars of the prospecting activity.

2. If a Party to this regime considers that any prospecting activity may be inconsistent with the provisions of this regime or, in the case of prospecting involving drilling or dredging or excavating for the purpose of taking samples or the establishment of a permanent or semi-permanent installation, present a hazard to the Antarctic environment against which adequate precautions are not being taken, it may, through a notification to the Secretariat, which shall be circulated without delay to the other Parties to the regime, request a review of the prospecting in question.

3. If [ ] other Parties inform the Secretariat that they support the request made, the Depositary shall within three months convene a meeting of the Commission to consider the matter.

4. Without prejudice to the authority vested in it by paragraph 5 of Article XXIV, the Commission, after receiving information from the sponsoring state concerned and if the circumstances warrant, may recommend measures to ensure consistency of the prospecting with

the provisions of the regime or, as the case may be, to reduce or eliminate any conflict with other uses of Antarctica or any environmental hazard.

5. In the event that the Commission decides to make a recommendation pursuant to paragraph 4 of this Article, the sponsoring state concerned shall submit within [   ] months a report to the Commission on its response to that recommendation.

6. Nothing in this Article shall derogate from the provisions of Chapter VII of this regime relating to the settlement of disputes.

Article XXIV (ter) (Expanded scope for Prospecting in an area which has been identified for Exploration and Development)

1. When an area has been identified pursuant to Article XXVI, the Commission may decide to apply the provisions of Articles XXIII, XXIV and XXIV (bis), subject to any conditions the Commission may establish pursuant to paragraph 5 of Article XXIV, to prospecting in the area involving off-structure drilling at a depth greater than that specified in Article I.

CHAPTER IV: (Exploration)

Article XXV (Notification)

1. A Party to the regime which has an interest in the exploration and development of a particular mineral resource may, at any time, submit a notification to the Secretariat requesting the Commission to make a determination authorizing the submission of applications for exploration and development of that mineral resource in respect of an identified area.

2. Such notification shall:
   (a) specify the area in respect of which the Party or an operator under its sponsorship has an interest in exploration and development;
   (b) provide information concerning the resource in respect of which the interest exists;
   (c) contain a detailed account of the physical and environmental conditions in the area;
   (d) specify the proposed methods of exploration and development;
   (e) provide an assessment of the impact on the environment of the proposed exploration and development and of the measures that would be adopted to avoid harmful consequences;
   (f) such further information as may be required in rules established by the Commission.

3. A notification under paragraph (1) shall be referred immediately to all members of the Commission and the Advisory Committee.

4. The Commission shall meet to consider the notification and shall refer it to the Advisory Committee with the request that it submit advice to the Commission within a prescribed time.

144

Article XXVI (Action by the Commission)

1. The Commission shall meet, as soon as practicable after the receipt of the advice of the Advisory Committee, to determine whether or not to authorize the submission of applications for exploration and development in respect of an identified area.

2. In making this determination the Commission shall take full account of the principles contained in Article II and Article III of this regime, and the advice tendered by the Advisory Committee. The Commission shall decline to make a positive determination in accordance with paragraph 1 of this Article if the exploration envisaged or subsequent development would present an unacceptable risk to the Antarctic environment. The Commission's determination may be conditional on the observance of requirements specified by the Advisory Committee, including the establishment, where appropriate, of closed areas within the area identified.

3. Any area identified by the Commission in accordance with paragraph 1 of this Article may include the whole or part of the area which was the subject of the notification submitted pursuant to paragraph 1 of Article XXV, and it may include adjacent areas not covered by that notification.

4. Any area identified by the Commission in accordance with paragraph 1 of this Article shall be such that, taking into account the physical, geological, environmental and other characteristics of the area, it can effectively be treated as a unit for the purpose of resource management.

5. The Commission shall also specify the mineral resource in respect of which applications for exploration and development may be submitted.

6. If, after a positive determination in accordance with this Article has been made, a Party to the regime submits a notification pursuant to Article XXV with respect to a different mineral resource but within the area already identified, that notification shall be dealt with in accordance with Article XXV and this Article should it decide to identify an area with respect to the newly requested mineral resource, the Commission shall have regard, in addition to the requirements of paragraph 4 of this Article, to the desirability of specifying the boundaries of the area in such a way that it can be assigned to the same Regulatory Committee already established as a consequence of the Commission's initial determination.

7. In the light of increased knowledge or other factors relating to the effective management of the area, and after seeking the views of the Advisory Committee, the Commission may amend the boundaries of any area it has identified. In making any such amendment the Commission shall ensure that existing exploration and development activities in the area are protected. Unless there are compelling reasons to do so, the Commission shall not amend an area it has identified in such a way as to involve, in terms of Article XX, a change in the

composition of the Regulatory Committee with competence in respect of that area.

8. Decisions of the Commission pursuant to this Article shall be taken by consensus.

Article XXVI (bis) (Preparatory Work by the Regulatory Committee)

1. Within [ ] months of a determination by the Commission pursuant to Article XXVI to authorize the submission of applications for exploration and development in an identified area, the Regulatory Committee with competence in respect of that area and constituted in accordance with Article XX shall be convened.

2. The Regulatory Committee shall:
   (a) subject to any rules established by the Commission pursuant to Article XIII(1) (a) relating to maximum block sizes, identify specific blocks within its area of competence in respect of which applications for exploration and development permits may be submitted;
   (b) subject to any rules established by the Commission pursuant to Article XII(1) (i) establish fees to be submitted with any application for an exploration or development permit pursuant to Articles XXVII and XXXIV.

3. Terms and Conditions/Guidelines/Indicative Guidelines.]
   [no formal proposals exist]

Article XXVII (Exploration Applications)

1. At any time after the expiry of 30 days from the date on which the Regulatory Committee has completed the action required of it by Article XXVI (bis), any Party, either on its own behalf or on behalf of an operator under its sponsorship may lodge with the Secretariat an application for an exploration permit.

2. Such an application shall:
   (a) provide details of the resource to be explored;
   (b) provide a detailed description of the exploration methods to be used including a description of installations, equipment and any support facilities, together with an account of the methods which will be used at the development stage;
   (c) contain a detailed assessment of the environmental impact of the proposed activities including support facilities;
   (d) contain a detailed statement of the measures to be taken to avoid harmful environmental consequences, including a detailed contingency plan to be put into effect in the event of any accident;
   (e) a description of the measures to be taken to guarantee the safety of installations and personnel;
   (f) specify the requested duration of the exploration permit;
   (g) in the area of exploration undertaken by an operator other than a Party, contain:

(i) a detailed description of the operator, including financial participation, and other evidence that it has a substantial and genuine link with the sponsoring state as required by Article V;

(ii) evidence that the operator has the necessary financial resources and technical expertise to ensure compliance with the provisions of this regime and measures adopted pursuant to it;

(h) such further information as may be required by rules established by the Commission.

Article XXVII (Examination of Applications)

1. Within [ ] days of the receipt by the Secretariat of an application under Article XXVII, the Regulatory Committee shall meet to consider the application. For that purpose it may, if it finds it necessary, seek further detailed information from the Party which submitted the application.

2. In the event that two or more applications are lodged in respect of the same block, they shall be dealt with in the order in which they were lodged with the Secretariat.

3. In the case of exploration to be undertaken by an operator other than a Party to the regime, the Regulatory Committee, if it is not satisfied that the requirements of Article V have been met or that the operator has the necessary financial resources and technical expertise to ensure compliance with the regime and any measures adopted pursuant to it, may decline to take any further action on the application.

4. Subject to paragraph 3 of this Article, the Regulatory Committee shall refer the application to the Advisory Committee for an assessment of it.

5. In assessing the application referred to it, the Advisory Committee shall;

(a) identify attendant environmental risks;

(b) identify means by which the risks of environmental damage might be reduced to a practical minimum;

(c) identify any residual environmental risks which, if the application were approved, would have to be accepted; and shall advise, in the light of all the information available to it, and on the basis of the principles of Article III and any relevant measures which may have been adopted by the Commission pursuant to Article XIII, whether the application, if approved, would or would not involve an unacceptable risk to the environment.

6. The advice tendered by the Advisory Committee shall also contain guidelines including:

(a) detailed measures for the protection of the environment;

(b) technical and safety standards and procedures;

(c) monitoring procedures;

(d) data collection and reporting requirements;

(e) contingency plan requirements;

(f) criteria for suspension, modification or cancellation of permits in the event of identification of unforseen risks to the environment.

7. The Advisory Committee shall present its advice to the Regulatory Committee within [ ] months of the applications being referred to it.

8. In the event that the Advisory Committee advises that the application, if approved, would involve an unacceptable risk to the environment, the Regulatory Committee shall either:

   (a) reject the application; or

   (b) refer the application to the Commission which may by [ ] authorize the Regulatory Committee to proceed with consideration of the application subject to such conditions as it sees fit.

9. In the event that the Advisory Committee considers that the application does not present an unacceptable risk to the Antarctic environment, the Regulatory Committee shall proceed with the preparation of a Management Scheme to cover both exploration and development which shall give effect to any relevant measures adopted by the Commission and take fully into account the guidelines established by the Advisory Committee.

Article XXIX (Management Scheme)

1. The Regulatory Committee shall designate one of its members to present a draft Management Scheme.

2. In appropriate cases the Regulatory Committee may designate more than one member to prepare a draft Management Scheme.

3. The designations referred to in paragraphs 1 and 2 of this Article shall be decided by a simple majority of the members of the Regulatory Committee, which majority shall include the members referred to in paragraph 3(a) and paragraph 4(b) of Article XX.

Article XXX (Scope of the Managements Scheme)

1. The draft Management Scheme shall prescribe terms and conditions relating to the following:

   (a) the law applicable to the operator and persons employed by the operator in connection with the proposed exploration and development activities:

   (b) arrangements for the grant of authorization to conduct activities;

   (c) inspection and enforcement of the Mangement Scheme;

   (d) levies payable by operators in accordance with Article XXIII(1) (j);

   (e) other financial obligations of operators including payments in the nature of taxes, royalties or payments in kind;

   (f) technical and safety specifications, including standards and procedures to ensure safe operation and full observance of the environmental principles set out in Arcticle III of this regime;

   (g) monitoring of all aspects of the exploration and development programs;

   (h) depletion policy;

148

(i)   time limits and diligence requirements during exploration;
(j)   duration of exploration permit;
(k)   data collection, reporting and notification requirements;
(l)   contingency plans and equipment to deal with accidents;
(m)   liability, bonding and insurance;
(n)   assignment or relinquishment of permits;
(o)   decommissioning requirements;
(p)   procedures for obtaining consent for modifications;
(q)   suspension, modification or cancellation of the Management
       Scheme in the event that the Regulatory Committee determines
       that there has been failure to comply with the provisions of the
       Management Scheme or that there are unforeseen risks to the
       environment.

Article XXXI (Adoption of the Management Scheme)

1. The draft Management Scheme shall be presented to the Regulatory
    Committee for approval by a simple majority, which majority shall
    include the members referred to in paragraph 3(a) and paragraph 4(b)
    of Article XX.
2. The Regulatory Committee shall refer the approved Management
    Scheme to the Commission.   Upon receipt, the Commission may
    adopt the Management Scheme and shall then authorize the issue of
    an exploration permit, in accordance with the Management Scheme.
3. In the event that the Commission fails to adopt the Management
    Scheme as referred by the Regulatory Committee, it shall be referred
    back to the Regulatory Committee for reconsideration in accordance
    with the procedures specified in Article XXIX.

Article XXXII (Rights of Approved Applicants)

1. An operator to which an exploration permit has been granted pursu-
    ant to Article XXXI shall have exclusive rights to explore and, subject
    to Article XXXIV and XXXV, to develop in respect of the block and the
    mineral resource to which that permit relates.
2. Such rights shall be subject to compliance with the regime and any
    measures adopted pursuant to it, including the approved Manage-
    ment Scheme.
3. Each operator to which an exploration or development permit has
    been granted pursuant to Article XXXI shall exercise its rights with due
    regard to the rights of other operators undertaking exploration or
    development in the same area identified pursuant to Article XXVI.

Article XXXIII (Montoring)

The Advisory Committee and the Regulatory Committee shall monitor the operator's compliance with a Management Scheme and report
thereon to the Commission on a regular basis.

CHAPTER V: (Development)

Article XXXIV (Notification of Application for Development Permit)

1. At any time during the period in which an approved Management Scheme and exploration permit are in force, the sponsoring state may lodge with the Secretariat an application for a development permit.
2. Such applications shall:
   (a) provide updated information in relation to all the matters specified in paragraph 2 of Article XXVII;
   (b) provide information on proposed modifications of any kind to the activities covered by the approved Management Scheme and any additional measures to be taken, consequent upon such modifications, to ensure the safety of the development activity and the protection of the Antarctic environment;
   (c) contain, in the case of development to be undertaken by an operator other than a Party updated information of the kind required by paragraph 2(g) of Article XXVII;
   (d) such further information as may be required in rules established by the Commission.
3. The Secretariat shall refer such applications to the Regulatory Committee and to the Advisory Committee.

Article XXXV (Review of Applications and Issue of Development Permits)

1. The Advisory Committee shall review any application referred to it pursuant to paragraph 3 of Article XXXIV and shall complete that review and report to the Regulatory Committee within [ ] months of the lodging of the notification with the Secretariat pursuant to paragraph 1 of Article XXXIV.
2. In reviewing any application the Advisory Committee shall determine whether;
   (a) it reveals any significant modifications to the development activities envisaged at the time the Management Scheme was adopted;
   (b) whether there are any significant modifications to the environmental considerations unforeseen at the time the Managment Scheme was adopted.
3. If the Advisory Committee determines that either of the conditions described in paragraph, 2 of this Article exist, it shall include, in its report to the Regulatory Committee, guidelines for the modification of the Management Scheme so as to ensure its continuing consistency with this regime, including the principles set out in Article III and any measures adopted by the Commission pursuant to Article XIII.
4. Within [ ] months of the receipt of the report of the Advisory Committee, the Regulatory Committee shall meet to consider that report. In the case that the Advisory Committee has determined that either of the conditions referred to in paragraph 2 of this Article exists, the Regulatory Committee shall make the necessary modification to the

Management Scheme and in so doing shall take full account of the guidelines proposed by the Advisory Committee. In no case shall such modification relate to the finanacial obligations specified in the Management Scheme.

5. The Regulatory Committee shall refer the original Management Scheme or the modified Management Scheme, as the case may be, to the Commission.

6. Upon reciept of the original or modified Management Scheme, the Commission shall, without futher review, authorize the issue of a development permit in accordance with it.

CHAPTER VI: (Links with International Organizations)

Article XXXVI (Cooperation with international organizations)

1. The Commision shall cooperate with the Antarctic Treaty Consultative Parties and the Commission for the Conservation of Antarctic Marine Living Resources in accordance with Article VIII.

2. The Commission shall also cooperate with:
   (a) the United Nations and its relevant specialized agencies;
   (b) the Scientific Committee on Antarctic Research, and the International Union for the Conservation of Nature;
   (c) any other relevant international organizations.

3. The Commission shall, as appropriate, seek to develop a cooperative working relationship with any international organization which may have competence in respect of mineral resources in areas adjacent to those covered by this regime.

4. The Commission may enter into agreements with the organiations referred to in this Article.

CHAPTER VII: (Dispute Settlement)
-to be elaborated.

BIBLIOGRAPHY

Primary Sources

Antarctic Treaty, "Final Report of the Eighth Antarctic Consultative Meeting", National Archives of the United States, Center for Polar Archives, Reference File.

Antarctic Treaty, "Final Report of the Fourth Antarctic Consultative Meeting", National Archives of the United States, Center for Polar Archives, Reference File.

Greenpeace International, "The Future of Antarctica: "Background for a Third UN Debate", 25 November 1985.

Permanent Court of International Justice, Ser. A/B, 53,3, Denmark v. Norway, 1933.

South Africa, "Antarctic Treaty Administrative Arrangements", National Archives of the United States, Center for Polar Archives, Record Group 307, Records of the National Science Foundation, Office of Antarctic Programs, Central Subject Files, Box 17, File 102D. Herafter such sources are listed, regardless of state of origin, by RG 307 with Box and File numbers.

United Kingdom, Foreign and Commonwealth Office, "Proposed Agreement on Conservation of Wildlife in the Antarctic", 28 February 1964, RG 307, Box 29, File 102D.

United Nations, *United Nations Reports of International Arbitrations and Awards, Vol. 2.* 1932, France v. Mexico.

United Nations, *United Nations Reports of International Arbitrations and Awards, Vol. 2.* Permanent Court of Arbitration, 1928, US v. Netherlands.

United Nations, First Committee, "Question of Antarctica", A/38/646.

United Nations, First Committee, "Question of Antarctica", A/C.11/39/L.83.

United Nations, General Assembly, "Question of Antarctica", A/Res/38/77.

United Nations, General Assembly, "Question of Antarctica", A/Res/40/156.

United Nations, Secretary General, "Question of Antarctica", A/39/583, Vols. I-III.

United States, Congress, *Congressional Record.* 8 August 1960, p. 15981.

United States, Department of State, *Conference on Antarctica.* (Washington, DC: Government Printing Office, 1960).

United States, Department of State, "Draft Position Paper on Administrative Arrangements", RG 307, Box 29, File 102.1.1. [First Consultative Meeting].

United States, Department of Sate, "Draft Position Paper on conservation of Antarctic Living Resources", RG 307, Box 29, File 102.1.1. [First Consultative Meeting].

United States, Department of State, "Draft Position Paper on Radio Communication in Antarctica", RG 307, Box 29, File 102.1.1. [First Consultative Meeting].

United States, Department of State, "Draft Position Paper on Relations with SCAR", RG 307, Box 29, File 102.1.1. [First Consultative Meeting].

United States, Department of State, "Draft Position Paper on the Exchange of Information on Scientific Programs", RG 307, Box 29, File 102.1.1. [First Consultative Meeting].

United States, Department of State, *Foreign Relations of the United States, 1939, Vol. 2.* (Washington,. DC: Government Printing Office, 1956).

United States, Department of State, *Foreign Relations of the United States, 1948, Vol. I, parts 2 and 3.* (Congressional Information Service, 1980, H920.5).

United States, Department of State, *Foreign Relations of the United States, 1949, Vol. I.* (Congressional Information Service, 1980, H920.10).

United States, Department of State, *Foreign Relations of the United States, 1951, Vol. I.* (Congressional Information Service, 1980, H920.26).

United States, Department of State, "General Comments on the Draft Fourth Consultative Meeting Preparatory Report", RG 307, Box 18, File 102D.

United States, Department of State, "Minutes of the First Preparatory Meeting for the Fifth Consultative Meeting", Enclosure to Airgram A-1076, US Embassy London to Department of State Washington, 26 December 1967, RG 307, Box 20, File 102D.

United States, Department of State, "Minutes of the Fourth Preparatory Meeting for the Fifth Consultative Meeting", Enclosure to Airgram-2426, US Embassy Paris to Department of State Washington, 26 July 1986, RG 307, Box 20, File 102D.

United States, Department of State, "Minutes of the Second Meeting in Preparation of the Third Antarctic Treaty Consultative Meeting", Enclosure to Airgram A-1262, US Embassy Brussels to Department of State Washington, 26 August 1963, RG 307, Box 18, File 102D.

United States, Department of State, "Notes on the Fifth Preparatory Meeting [for the Fifth Consultative Meeting]", Letter to James Simsarian from John H. Buehler, Assistant Scientific Attaché, US Embassy Paris, 22 September 1968, RG 307, Box 20, File 102D.

United States, Department of State, "Points Inscrits à L'Ordre du Jour de la 3ème Réunion Consultative de Bruxelles", Enclosure Two to Airgram A-1095, US Embassy Brussels to Department of State Washington, May 1964, RG 307, Box 17, File 102D.

United States, Department of State, "Position Paper for the Fourth Consultative Meeting: Chilean Amendments to the Agreed Measures", National Archives of the United States, Center for Polar Archives, Record Group 313, Records of Naval Operating Forces, US Naval Support Force, Antarctica. Historical and Research Divison, Research Files, Reprints and Publications, Box 80, File 2A112. Hereafter such records will be cited by RG 313 with Box and File numbers.

United States, Department of State, "Position Paper for the Fourth Consultative Meeting: Coordination of Permits", RG 313, Box 80, File 2A112.

United States, Department of State, "Position Paper for the Fourth Consultative Meeting: Declassification of Official Records of the Antarctic Conference and Consultative Meetings", 1 June 1966, RG 307, Box 18, File 102D.

United States, Department of State, "Position Paper for the Fourth Consultative Meeting: Implementation of Article XIII, (1) (d) of the Agreed Measures", RG 313, Box 80, File 2A112.

United States, Department of State, "Position Paper for the Fourth Consultative Meeting: Meetings of Experts", 26 October 1966, RG 313, Box 80, File 2A112.

United States, Department of State, "Position Paper for the Fourth Consultative Meeting: Meeting of Experts on Logistics", Draft Version, 19 May 1966, RG 307, Box 18, File 102D.

United States, Department of State, "Position Paper for the Fourth Consultative Meeting: Pelagic Sealing", RG 313, Box 80, File 2A112.

United States, Department of State, "Position Paper for the Fourth Consultative Meeting: Recommendations of the Consultative Meetings", 27 October 1966, RG 313, Box 80, File 2A112.

United States, Department of State, "Position Paper on Amending the Agreed Measures", RG 307, Box 20, File 102D [Fifth Consultative Meeting].

United States, Department of State, "Position Paper on the Coordination of SCAR General Meetings and the Consultative Meetings", RG 307, Box 20, File 102D [Fifth Consultative Meeting].

United States, Department of State, "Position Papers of the United States for the Third Consultative Meeting", RG 313, Box 79, File 2A112.

United States, Department of State, "Preparatory Delegation Report" RG 307, Box 18, File 102D [Fourth Consultative Meeting Preparations].

United States, Department of State, "Procès-Verbal de la Troisème Réunion Préparatoire à la IIIe Réunion Consultative de L'Antarctique", Enclosure to Airgram A-17, US Embassy Brussels to Department of State Washington, 5 July 1963, RG 307, Box 18, File 102D.

United States, Department of State, "Procès-Verbal de la 5ème Réunion Préparatoire à la IIIe Réunion de L'Antarctique", Enclosure to Airgram A-606, US Embassy Brussels to Department of State Washington, 23 December 1963, RG 307, Box 18, File 102D.

United States, Department of State, "Procès-Verbal de la 6ème Réunion Préparatoire à la IIIe Réunion Consultative", Enclosure to Airgram A-743, US Embassy Brussels to Department of State Washington, January 1964, RG 307, Box 18, File 102D.

United States, Department of State, "Procès-Verbal de la 7ème Réunion Préparatoire à la IIIe Réunion Consultative", Enclosure to Airgram A-981, US Embassy Brussels to Department of State Washington, 6 March 1964, RG 307, Box 18, File 102D.

United States, Department of State, "Procès-Verbal de la 8ème Réunion Préparatoire a la IIIe Réunion Consultative," Enclosure to Airgram A-1070, US Embassy Brussels to Department of State Washington, 30 April 1964, RG 307, Box 18, File 102D.

United States, Department of State, "Procès-Verbal de la 9ème Réunion Préparatoire a la IIIe Réunion Consultative," Enclosure to Airgram A-1090, US Embassy Brussels to Department of State Washington, May 1964, RG 307, Box 18, File 102D.

United States, Department of State, "Report of the US Delegation to the Fourth Consultative Meeting: Agreed Measures for the Conservation of Antarctic Fauna and Flora", RG 307, Box 19, File 102D.

United States, Department of State, "Report of the US Delegation to the Fourth Consultative Meeting: Coordination of Permits", RG 307, Box 19, File 102D.

United States, Department of State, "Report of the US Delegation to the Fourth Consultative Meeting: Exchange of Information", Draft Version, RG 307, Box 19, File 102D.

United States, Department of State, "Report of the US Delegation to the Fourth Consultative Meeting: Implementation of Article XIII (1) (d) of the Agreed Measues", RG 307, Box 19, File 102D.

United States, Department of State, "Report of the US Delegation to the Fourth Consultative Meeting: Meeting of Experts on Logistics", Draft Version, 19 May 1966, RG 307, Box 18, File 102D.

United States, Department of State, "Report of the US Delegation to the Fourth Consultative Meeting: Meetings of Experts", RG 307, Box 19, File 102D.

United States, Department of State, "Report of the US Delegation to the Fourth Consultative Meeting: Pelagic Sealing", RG 307, Box 19, File 102D.

United States, Department of State, "Report of the US Delegation to the Fourth Consultative Meeting: Place and Date of Next Meeting", RG 307, Box 19, File 102D.

United States, Department of State, "Report of the US Delegation to the Fifth Consultative Meeting under Article IX of the Antarctic Treaty," RG 307, Box 20, File 102D.

United States, Department of State, "Report of the US Delegation to the Third Consultative Meeting under the Antarctic Treaty," RG 307, Box 18, File 102D.

United States, Department of State, "Soviet Draft Regulations on Flora and Fauna", July 1962, RG 313, Box 29, File 102.1.

United States, Department of State, Telegram 915, 830A. From US Embassy Canberra to US Information Agency Washington, 14 July 1961, RG 307, Box 29, File 102.1.1.

United States, Department of State, Division of Language Services, "Minutes of the First Preparatory Meeting for the Third Antarctic Treaty Consultative Meeting", LS no. RXV-RXVIII in French, RG 307, Box 29, File 102.1.

United States, Department of State, Division of Language Services, "Minutes of the Fourth Meeting in Preparation for the Third Antarctic Consultative Meeting", LS no. 8421, T-39, R-XVIII in French, RG 307, Box 18, File 102D.

United States, Department of State, Division of Language Services, "Notes on the Draft Convention for the Conservation of Live Resources of Antarctica", LS no. 58420, T-21/R-13, Russian, RG 307, Box 18, File 102D.

United States, National Science Foundation, "Memorandum from Henry S. Francis to Charles Maechling", 19 February 1969, RG 307, Box 20, File 102D.

United States, National Science Foundation, "Trip Report to the First Antartcic Treaty Consultative Meeting" RG 307, Box 29, File 102.1.2.

United States, National Science Foundation, "Trip Report to the Second Consultative Meeting", RG 307, Box 29, File 102.1.

United States, Senate, Committee on Foreign Relations, "Antarctic Treaty", Hearings, 86th Congress, 2nd Session, 1960.

United States, Senate, Committee on Foreign Relations, Subcommittee on Oceans and International Environment, "US Antarctic Policy", 94th Congress, 1st Session, 1975.

United States, United States Navy, "Memorandum for the Record on the Second Consultative Meeting", RG 313, Box 79, File 2A112.

Books and Pamphlets

Aramayo Alzerreca, Carlos, *História de la Antártida.* (Buenos Aires: Editorial Hemisferio, 1949).

Auburn, F.M., *Antarctic Law and Politics.* (London: C. Hurst and Company, 1982).

Auburn, F.M., *The Ross Dependency.* (The Hague: Martinus Nijhoff, 1972).

Bertrand, Kenneth J., *Americans in Antarctica, 1775-1948.* (New York: American Geographical Society, 1971).

Friedman, Wolfgang G., Oliver J. Lissitzyn and Richard Crawford Pugh, (eds.), *Cases and Materials on International Law.* (St. Paul, Minnesota: West Publishing Company, 1969).

Friedrich, Christof, *Germany's Antarctic Claim: Secret Nazi Polar Expeditions.* (Toronto: Samisdat Publishers, Ltd., 1978).

Hackworth, G.H., *Digest of International Law, Vol. I.* (Washington, DC: Government Printing Office, 1940).

Jennings, R.Y., *The Acquisition of Territory in International Law.* (Manchester: Manchester University Press, 1963).

Jessup, Philip C. and Howard J. Taubenfeld, *Control for Outer Space and the Antarctic Analogy.* (New York: Columbia University Press, 1959).

Lauterpacht, H., *Annual Digest of Public International Law Cases: 1931-32.* (London: Longmans, Green and Company, 1935).

McNair, Arnold D., and H. Lauterpacht, *Annual Digest of Public International Law Cases: 1927-28.* (London: Longmans, Green and Company,

156

1931).

Mendez, Armando Braun, *Pequeña História Antárctica*. (Buenos Aires: Editorial Francisco de Aquirre, S.A., 1974).

Myhre, Jeffrey D., *The Antarctic Treaty Consultative Meetings, 1961-68: A Case Study in Cooperation, Compliance and Negotiation in the International System*. (PhD dissertation: London School of Economics and Political Science, December 1983).

Plott, B.M., *The Development of United States Antarctic Policy*. (PhD dissertation: Fletcher School of Law and Diplomacy, Tufts University, 1969).

Quartermain, L.B., *New Zealand and the Antarctic*. (Wellington: New Zealand Government Printers, 1971).

Quigg, Philip W., *A Pole Apart: The Emerging Issue of Antarctica*. (New York: McGraw Hill Book Company, 1983).

Ross, Frank J., jr., *Partners in Science: The Story of the International Geophysical Year*. (New York: Lothrop, Lee and Shepard, Co., Inc., 1960).

Sullivan, W., *Quest for a Continent*. (New York: McGraw Hill Book Company, 1957).

Sullivan, Walter, *Assault on the Unknown: The International Geophysical Year*. (New York: McGraw Hill Book Company, 1961).

Whiteman, M.M., *Digest on International Law, Vol. II*. (Washington, DC: Government Printing Office, 1963).

Periodicals and Interviews

American Journal of International Law. (Vol. 26, 1932).

ECO (Vol. XX, Nos. 1-3, 14-25, June 1982; Vol. XXII, Nos. 1-3, 17-28 January 1983; Vol. XXIII, No. 1, July 1983; Vol. XXVI, Nos. 1-2, 18-27 January 1984; Vol. XXVII, No. 2, 22-31 May 1984; Vol. XXXIII, No. 2, 23 September-4 October 1985; Vol. XXXIV, Nos. 1-2, 7-18 October 1985).

Polar Record. (Vol. 5, No. 35), pp. 241-43.

"India Establishes Foothold in Antarctica", *Washington Post*. 2 February 1983, p. A16.

Interview with R. Tucker Scully, Director of the Office of Oceans and Polar Affairs, United States' Department of State, 10 February 1983.

"Report on the Sixth Consultative Meeting, Tokyo, 1970", *Polar Record*. (Vol. 15, No. 98), pp. 729-42.

"Russian Base in the Antarctic: Australian Concern", *The Times* (London). 7 February 1957, p. 7.

"US Maps Formal Claims", *New York Times*. 6 January 1957, p. 21.

Bertram, G.C.L., "Antarctic Prospect", *International Affairs*. (Vol. 33, No. 2, April 1957), pp. 143-8.

Hayton, Robert D., "The 'American' Antarctic", *American Journal of International Law*. (Vol. 50, July 1956), pp. 583-610.

Hayton, Robert D., "The Antarctic Settlement of 1959", *American Journal of International Law*. (Vol. 54, 1960), pp. 349-71.

Myhre, Jeff, "What Not to Do about Antarctic Mineral Rights", *Wall Street Journal (Europe)*. 21 July 1983, p. 10.

Myhre, Jeffrey D., "Title to the Falkland-Malvinas Islands under International Law", *Millennium: Journal of International Studies*. (Vol. 12, No. 1, Spring 1983), pp. 25-38.

SCAR, *Polar Record*. (Vol. 14, No. 92, May 1969), pp. 670-5.

Spivak, Jonathan, "Frozen Assets" *Wall Street Journal*. 21 February 1974, *passim*.

Sullivan, Walter, "Antarctica in a Two-Power World", *Foreign Affairs*. (October 1957), pp. 154-66.

Taubenfeld, Howard J., "A Treaty for Antarctica", *International Conciliation*. (January 1961), pp. 249-55.

Toma, Peter A., "The Soviet Attitude toward the Acquisition of Territorial Sovereignty in Antarctica", *American Journal of International Law*. (Vol. 50, July 1956), pp. 611-26.

INDEX

162